Travels of an American Girl

by June Potter Durkee

The Historical Series of the Reformed Church in America
No. 45

Travels of an American Girl

by June Potter Durkee

Wm. B. Eerdmans Publishing Co.
Grand Rapids, Michigan

© Copyright 2004 Reformed Church Press
All Rights Reserved

Wm. B. Eerdmans Publishing Co.
255 Jefferson Avenue, S.E., Grand Rapids, Michigan 49503
P.O. Box 163 Cambridge CB3 9PU U.K.

Printed in the United States of America

Library of Congress Cataloging-in-publication Data

Durkee, June Potter
          Travels of an American Girl / June Potter Durkee
          p. cm. - (Historical Series of the Reformed Church in America, no. 45)
          ISBN 0-8028-2869-8
1. Reformed Church in America, Mission History. 2. Reformed Church in America,
Missions in Egypt, Iraq, Kuwait, Bahrain, Muscat, India. 3. Travel: England, France,
Lebanon, Egypt, Iraq, Kuwait, Bahrain, Muscat, India.

The Historical Series of the Reformed Church in America

The series was inaugurated in 1968 by the General Synod of the Reformed Church in America acting through the Commission on History to communicate the church's heritage and collective memory and to reflect on our identity and mission, encouraging historical scholarship which informs both church and academy.

General Editor
    The Rev. Donald J. Bruggink, Ph.D.
    Western Theological Seminary

Commission on History
    James Hart Brumm, M.Div., Blooming Grove, New York
    Lynn Japinga, Ph.D., Hope College, Holland, Michigan
    Scott M. Manetsch, Ph.D., Trinity Seminary, Deerfield, Illinois
    Melody Meeter, M.Div., Brooklyn, New York
    Jesus Serrano, B.A., Norwalk, California
    Robert Terwilliger, M.Div., Kalamazoo, Michigan

Contents

Illustrations

Acknowledgements

I am so grateful to my friend, Laurie Lee Clayton, who first discovered my almost-forgotten diary. Taking it with her to her home in Florida, she transcribed and compiled the childishly handwritten pages into the computer. Without her hard work and interest, its yellowed pages would probably still be in my attic.

I am also indebted to the Reverend Al Poppen, who first read the manuscript on a plane to Chicago. His enthusiastic efforts resulted in its being approved for publication.

Finally, I am grateful to Russ Gasero whose tireless efforts culminated in getting the final manuscript to the publishers.

Foreword

One day, as Jesus' disciples argued about which of them was the greatest, he drew a child to his side and said, "Whoever welcomes this child in my name welcomes me." (Luke 9:48). On another occasion, before blessing the children around him, he remarked, "it is to such as these that the kingdom of God belongs" (Mark 10:14).

In *Travels of an American Girl* we meet some of the legendary giants in Reformed Church mission history, as seen through the eyes of a precocious ten-year-old girl. June Potter had little awareness of their achievements, but she was an astute observer of how they lived their daily lives and related to her. They not only welcomed her, mostly she found them "swell"—which seems to have been the 1938 equivalent of today's "cool." The towering John Badeau finds time and inclination to write a poem for her; the John VanEss home soon seems like her own; Paul Harrison takes her on wild rides through the desert; Cornelius DeBruin quickly becomes her "Uncle Corny"; and she plays game after game of pick-up-sticks with Ida Scudder.

Possibly not so well remembered today but a major figure in Reformed Church mission policy and administration for over thirty

years was June's own father, F. M. (Duke) Potter, secretary of the
Board of Foreign Missions until his death in 1952. Today he is cred-
ited with maintaining the financial stability of the RCA mission
enterprise through the very difficult Depression years and remembered as a genius with a mind that was a "cavernous and well-orga-
nized file" (Lewis Scudder III, *The Arabian Mission's Story*, p. 387). In
these pages he is simply "Daddy," perpetually scurrying after the
luggage, finding hotels that satisfy the more exacting standards of
his wife, going to meetings "all the time," and doing what good
dads do.

This book offers a snapshot of part of the extensive Reformed
Church mission enterprise in 1938-39. It was arguably the high-
water mark in a "foreign mission" tradition that began in the early
nineteenth century but changed forever following World War II. In
1938, mission was still "over there," defined by crossing salt water.
The great missionary institutions had reached maturity. Hospitals,
clinics, colleges, schools, and agricultural institutes were still funded
largely from overseas and led by foreign personnel. All that was
about to change as World War II ushered in an end to colonialism,
the rise of nationalism, and indigenous churches that had come of
age. As June Potter tells her story, the clouds of that war already
loom on the horizon, though the winds of change are not yet even
a breeze.

From today's perspective, it is difficult not to be just a little nos-
talgic for the gracious, unhurried lifestyle we find in these pages.
What mission executive could now conceive of visiting the area of
his or her responsibility only once in ten years? What missionary
could imagine a seven-year term of service before coming back to
raise support funds? Leisurely ocean voyages, months away from
the office with no e-mail, mission picnics, tennis games—all are
unthinkable for the "four-countries-in-three-weeks" schedules
which are now routine simply because they are possible.

Enter then, a lost world that will not return but is worth remem-
bering.

Al Poppen
March 2004

Introduction

My father, Dr. F. Marmaduke Potter, was the first Rhodes scholar from Rutgers University. Returning home in 1911 from Oxford after three years of study in England, he entered New Brunswick Theological Seminary in New Jersey to study for the ministry.

After two years, however, the mission board of the Dutch Reformed Church (now the Reformed Church in America) asked him to go to India to become the principal of Voorhees College in Vellore, eighty miles west of Madras. This he did at age twenty-eight, becoming the youngest principal ever to serve at that institution.

After only a year there, he sent a telegram back home to a very surprised young woman, who would later be my mother, declaring that he was coming back to the United States to marry her. This he did.

After a whirlwind courtship of only a few weeks, they were married in 1915 and then made the long and sometimes harrowing trip back by ship via the Pacific. From Rangoon to India, their ship zig-zagged to escape German submarines, which were rumored to be searching for British vessels carrying cargo.

My parents then spent two additional years in Vellore until my
father contracted malaria and was forced to return to the States.
Very shortly thereafter he was asked to become secretary of the
Board of Foreign Missions, as it was then called. In those days board
secretaries made the long journey by boat to visit the mission fields
only once every ten years. So it was that the year that I was ten years
old this story took place. It was the first time back in twenty years
for my mother and her very first trip to Europe.

All of my life since making this trip to India, about which you
will read, I have lived with its happy memories. From time to time
some small event, a snatch of conversation, a picture in the news or
even a smell would suddenly waft me back in an instant to that
time and place, which otherwise seemed to exist only in the memories of my parents and me.

Occasionally an item in the news would trigger a vivid picture in
my mind. With the onset of Desert Storm, and the more recent war
in Iraq, long forgotten names like Basra, Bahrain, and Kuwait
evoked images of hot desert sands, camel caravans, and, at night,
hundreds of pockets of flames glowing from out of the ground so
rich with "black gold." Then would come an impression of a stern-
faced Arab sheik breaking into laughter during dinner at the palace.

With the recent commemorations of the end of World War II fifty
years ago, I recalled again watching workmen dig up the parks in
London in preparation for a war that many felt to be imminent.
Also, I realized that names like Chamberlain, De Ladier, Mussolini,
and Hitler were very much a part of my young life in the autumn of
1938. Arriving home in the summer of 1939, we were only a couple
of months ahead of Germany's march into Poland in September of
that year.

To a child, all the circumstances of that trip seemed fairly com-
monplace. Until then, I had little knowledge of the world geographi-
cally and was even rather vague as to where India was, or any other
country, for that matter. My main concern at the time was finding
enough friends my age to play with along the way.

When I was twelve years old, again encouraged by my parents, I started to write a book about my experiences, borrowing heavily in style from the works of Carolyn Keene and Laura Lee Hope, who were my favorite authors at the time. Throughout my adventures I saw myself as a heroine from the Nancy Drew mysteries or even as one of the Bobsey Twins. My library enthusiasm began with our stay in England during a very tense period before World War II and waned when the narrative reached Marseilles.

From that date on, my diary picks up where the story leaves off. What follows is an account of that trip as seen through the eyes of a ten-year old, with a few explanations added to help clarify some of the people and events.

June Potter Durkee
Lincolnville, Maine

DATE *Sept. 22, 1938*

PLACE *London*

This morning we drove to Buckingham Palace and watched the changing of the guard in their brilliant costumes. As we watched a car drove through the gate and Queen Mary got out!

In the afternoon went to the Tower of London. It was fascinating. There were beefeaters all around. We saw the crown jewels and the room where the two little princes were kept prisoner also saw many dark gloomy dungeons and corridors — old armor guns.

We had tea in a little tea room across from the Tower.

DATE . Jan. 21, 1939

PLACE Vellore.

The DeBruuns drove us
back to Vellore early
in the morning.
This is "college Day"
at Voorhes College. Daddy
was at college all day
visiting with old
students.
mommy and I joined
them at lunch in
the High school.
We went back again
for tea and had our
pictures taken. In
the evening Daddy
& mommy went to Dr. Ida's
for dinner.

XV

Part I

The Book

Skyscrapers and Mud Huts:
My Trip to India At Age Ten
Written in 1940 at age Twelve

by June Potter Durkee

1
At Home on a Ship

I stared in utter amazement at my mother and father smiling so calmly before me.

"To India?!" I repeated as if to assure myself that I had heard correctly.

"That's right!" replied my father smiling more broadly than ever.

Thus reassured that I was actually going to far off India in only a few months, I began to "cut capers" about the upstairs hall like a wild Indian. (I was just ten at the time.)

The next day I trotted happily off to school gloating over the surprise in store for my school mates. I waylaid the first friend I came upon in the schoolyard and proceeded to tell her that I was going abroad to Europe, Arabia, Egypt, Syria, India, etc., etc. I talked and talked of all the wonderful places I was going to visit and all the remarkable things I would see. When I had finished my glowing descriptions I stood back triumphantly to see my friend's reactions. For a moment she stared at me wide-eyed and then said in an awed voice—"Gee, don't you wish you really were!"

I felt like a pricked balloon, but nevertheless I stalked in and told my story to my teacher who believed me. In the afternoon my mother came to school to verify my statements. Arrangements were made with my principal and with the teacher whom I was to have had the next year, and all agreed that a trip abroad would be well worth the lessons lost.

However, my mother armed herself with an English book, history book, and, alas, an arithmetic book to take with us in order to keep up with my lessons on the way. A geography book was obviously not needed.

The last few weeks in school I spent walking on air, likewise the following three months which fairly flew by due to the extensive packing and planning to be done.

In fact, the steamship tickets to England had been bought and passage arranged long before either my mother or I had even dreamed of such a trip. My mother and father had both been abroad, but this was my first experience of this sort and I was very excited indeed.

I spent most of my time looking over the various pamphlets from the different steamship companies. I never tired of going over and over the diagrams of the ship and seeing just where our cabin was located. My father had our itinerary all planned. Among the countries we were to visit were England, France, Holland, Germany, Switzerland, Italy, Egypt, Greece, Syria, Iraq, Arabia, and India. All these names fascinated me, although my sense of the general locations of the countries was a trifle blurred at the time.

I won't relate the happenings during the months before we sailed, but will merely start with that exciting day of Friday, September the 9th, 1938. We drove with my two big brothers, Allen and "Duke" to Pier 60 in New York where our boat, the *American Trader* was docked. A handful of relatives and friends had also come to see us off and bid us bon voyage. We all waited till my father had finished scurrying hither and thither making sure our baggage was intact and on board and that our passports were still in his possession. (We were to discover that each departure thereafter would be pre-

June with her parents and brothers, Francis and Allen

ceded by my father's scurries.) Then, we all went on board to look
the boat over.

It was somewhat small with all one class, but as the captain later
told my father, he carried "the cream of the Atlantic travel" on board.
My brothers were rather envious as they toured the ship, looking at
the foyer, the lounge, dining room, and our neat little white cabin,
for they were to spend the winter together at college while we were
sailing the seven seas on the *American Trader*.

We were due to sail at four o'clock, but supper came and we still
had not heard any warning whistle. So we went down to the dining
room to get a bite to eat while my brothers and relatives dashed
away for a sandwich and a cup of coffee. It was not until seven
o'clock that we heard the shrill warning whistle, the throbbing of
the engines, and the cry, "All ashore 'oos going ashore!"

Goodbyes were said, and my brothers, relatives, and the few re-
maining friends scurried down the gang-plank and stood on the
pier. The gang-plank was then drawn back on the deck. The engines gave a shudder and slowly we began to move out of the dock.

As we passed by the pier my brothers rushed along with us to the
tip of it. Slowly their figures grew smaller and smaller as we sailed

out into New York harbor. We stood on deck with the others on the boat and waved until we could no longer see them.

The lights along the shore were all lit and twinkling now, so we went up to the top deck and sat watching the shore-line and the dark buildings outlined against the sky. The lights and shore were still visible when we went down to our cabin at about eleven o'clock. Our cabin, I might add, was by this time just about bursting its sides with boxes of candy, books, magazines, flowers, and what-nots.

2
Over the Waves to England

The first morning I awoke to the steady throb of the engines and the lapping of the waves against the side of the ship. Our cabin was right up at the front of the ship and we could look out our porthole and see the sun shining down on the sea. There was no land in sight now and the ocean stretching out on all sides was just beautiful in the morning sunlight.

We spent the day up on the sun deck making acquaintances. I with an American girl who was going to school in England, and my parents with a group of eligible bridge players. The girl (Jean) and I played darts and sat in deck chairs watching the sea.

There was a boy here who reminded me of my brothers. He played the piano by ear and did magic tricks. He was English and his name was "Tibby."

The second day out to sea, I woke early. I got up, dressed quickly, and ate breakfast by myself in the dining room. When I went up on deck who should I bump into but the captain. He was very nice. We walked the deck together and talked.

The American Trader *U. S. Lines, N. Y. to Liverpool*

Those nine days at sea were glorious. The second day all the deck games were brought out on the sun deck. I loved playing deck tennis more than anything else. My father and mother played shuffle board quite often with a Baron and Baroness Von Something-or-other.

I noticed on about the sixth day out my father's brow began to darken every time he would go into the foyer and see the wireless messages just in with the latest news. It seems some man named Hitler was causing quite a stir in Europe and England wasn't quite as safe as it might be.

Every day was filled with all kinds of deck sports and every night there was some kind of entertainment in the lounge for everyone, old or young. Jean and I would get up games of hide-and-seek in and out and round the decks. Two English boys, also on their way back to England to school, would join us in our frolics. Tonight we saw the movie *Ruggles of Red Gap* with Charles Laughton.

The sixth day out it was rough, and Daddy and I stayed in our bunks, skipping lunch and breakfast. We told Mama with sickly grins, not to mind us but to go up on deck and enjoy the glorious sea air. If she wanted it, she could have it, we said. This she did, and spent the morning walking the decks without a qualm. Daddy and I have never lived this down. However, we were up in the afternoon and out on deck. The sea air quite restored us to our normal selves.

The night before we landed, a big masquerade was given and everyone appeared in the lounge attired in every kind of costume imaginable, scraped together from whatever materials they could find among their luggage. One man came as "the spirit of sea-sickness" draped with bottles of aspirin, sal hepatica, "Aunt Jenny's seasick remedy" and so forth. I dressed as a cigarette girl and won first prize, much to my astonishment.

On the morning of September 18 we caught sight of the coast of England and within a few hours we were passing the stately white cliffs of Dover. Then on slowly up the Thames, with everyone crowding the rails to see glimpses of the English countryside. My friends and I watched. They were all going to school in England. There was hardly time to say goodbye but Tibby gave me a box of candy. Imagine! At about noon we had dropped anchor at the Tilbury docks.

3
We Dock in London

A little boat took us on shore where Papa immediately began his scurries while Mama and I sat in the station (which was right by the docks) and waited for him. He dashed feverishly to and fro, making sure that no piece of luggage had gone astray or been left behind and when he was finally convinced that everything was well under control, he came over to us mopping his brow and told us that we were just in time to catch the train for London. We enjoyed watching from our train window the rows of little houses stretching along side by side, each with its own lovely little compact garden in the rear.

We arrived in London in the late afternoon and were directed by our taxi driver to the Hotel Imperial. How we would love to get that taxi driver—by the neck!

The minute my mother stepped into the lobby she declared that it looked more like Sing Sing than any hotel she'd ever seen. The lobby was like a huge dark cave. With difficulty we groped our way to the desk and Daddy got us a room. The upstairs was as bad or worse than the downstairs. Our room was large, to say the least, and like the downstairs—dark. Three beds stood along the side of one wall and the rest of the furniture looked as if it had been dumped in the room centuries before and somebody had forgotten to arrange it.

When we had drawn aside the heavy red draperies from three large windows we could see the roof of our hotel and also some pipes. I expected any minute to see Douglas Fairbanks come skipping lightly over the roof tops and into our window. Mama said she wouldn't open the bureau drawers if someone had a gun in her back, she was that sure that mice were in them. In the corner cowered a wash basin half concealed by the aforementioned draperies, as if hiding from its American visitors. The bathroom was way down the hall.

"Horrors!" said my mother. We plunked down our luggage in the middle of the floor and then left as rapidly as possible.

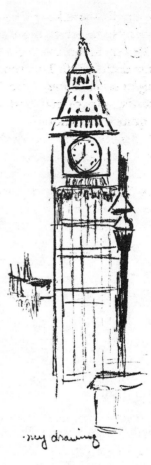

·my drawing·

On our first night in London we had dinner at the English-speaking Union. It was a lovely place and a lovely dinner. Mommy beamed all through the meal. After we had finished dinner we walked all through the beautiful building. Whenever anyone caught sight of my small figure their eyebrows would raise for just a speck, as children were not allowed in the place, generally. I was to learn that in England children were definitely seen and not heard and most of the time not even the former. We spent as long a time as possible in the English-speaking Union so as to delay as far as we could our inevitable return to our musty sleeping quarters.

We were forced to eat our breakfast the next morning in the hotel's huge dining hall. This room looked like a picture right out of my *Knights of the Round Table*. The dark walls were covered with old swords, suits of mail and armor, etc. The breakfast turned out to be quite good, though.

My mother and I spent the morning together while Daddy went off somewhere on business. We took a "two penny" bus and rode about the city. I was surprised that it really was so different from New York. In the first place, I missed seeing the tall skyscrapers—there were none here. I never got used to riding on the left hand side of the road, either. Out of our bus windows we could see tiny, crooked, cobblestone streets with old fashioned lamp posts branching off from the main thoroughfares. Mama whispered to me that her main intention in taking this morning ride was to find a different hotel.

And sure enough, we got off in front of a beautiful hotel that looked as if it had been shipped straight in from New York. The inside was just as beautiful. It was very modernistic and had mirrors all over the ceiling. The woman at the desk told us that if we could wait and come back in the afternoon we might be able to get a room.

When we got back to our hotel Daddy was waiting for us with a lovely couple—Mr. and Mrs. Peers, who took us to Westminster Abbey where they proved wonderful guides in taking us into every nook and corner of that famous cathedral. We saw everything from "Bloody Mary's" tomb to the old coronation chair. When we had finished our tour Mr. and Mrs. Peers took us to an Indian restaurant for a real Indian dish—rice and curry. It was a good thing I liked it for I was to have plenty before many months were up.

On our way back to the Hotel Imperial we told Papa of finding this new hotel. He did not say a word, but when we got to the Strand Palace (the name of the hotel) to show it to him he admitted that it was rather nice, and what's more, we found that the room was available. Our trouble lay in trying to switch hotels. But after a heated argument between our hotel manager and Papa, we found ourselves, bag and baggage, in the beautiful lobby of the Strand Palace.

Mama and I again spent the morning on penny buses riding all over the city and also walking up and down the main streets and looking in shop windows. The latter we found quite different from our own smartly planned windows on Fifth Avenue. Nearly every dress in the windows looked the same—tailored and straight, with only a little variety in the more expensive ones. Everyone along the streets seemed to be in no particular hurry and all moved along at a good easy pace—startling in contrast with New York streets where everyone dashes along in drastic danger of cracking one another's skulls. The longer we stayed in London the more we liked it.

We spent the afternoon with Daddy visiting Saint Paul's cathedral. I was especially impressed with the whispering gallery at the top of the cathedral where you could whisper a word to the circular wall and someone away on the other side could hear it. It was a very lovely place.

Daddy told us that during the morning he had met Governor and Mrs. Moore of New Jersey who happened to be in England at the time. He told us that both the governor and his wife were leaving London on the very next boat because of the ever increasing crisis of war in England. "The Gov." thought Daddy was crazy not sending my mother and me back to America at once, in fact everyone we met told us the same thing, but Daddy would calmly tell them that he was sure the crisis would pass over soon. At any rate, we did not leave on the next boat.

4

We Visit the Edgars in Ashsted

It rained the next day, but just the same this did not squelch our tourist instincts, so we took a bus to Buckingham Palace to see the changing of the guard. It would never do to go back to America and say we hadn't seen this famous sight. Besides, what better time to see it than in a London shower? It was a very impressive sight to see. The guards all wore bright red uniforms with large brass buttons and tall plumed hats. Some rode on horse-back but most of them marched with straight precision in long ranks. As we watched, a large black car drove up through the gates and on up to the front door of the palace, and who should step out but Queen Mary, the Queen Mother herself!

We had lunch at a tiny little restaurant nearby. When I asked the waitress for some tomato juice, she looked at me and said—

"No, no Miss—Now that your are in England you mustn't say to-*may*-to juice, you must say to-*mah*-to juice," and she smiled and scurried away.

In the afternoon we took a bus all the way to the tower of London. My, how I loved that place. It was so full of a "Henry the Eighth's" atmosphere with its musty dungeon cells and long, dark halls and even the old "chopping block" where so many queens were beheaded. At the door of the tower were two "beefeaters." In fact they were all around the tower, inside and out, with their quaint red costumes and long spears.  One of the main attractions of the tower was the jewel room in which were kept the crown jewels. The jewels were enclosed in a huge case in the tower. There were the king and queen's crowns, the princesses' coronets and the beautiful scepter with its huge red ruby on the end, and several other royal jewels all encased in a large glass container. Next, we saw the rooms where the little princes were kept prisoner and many dark, gloomy dungeons and corridors.

We had tea at a little old tea shop just across from the tower and then took the bus back to our hotel.

The next morning Daddy received an invitation from an old college friend of his for us to come and spend the weekend with him and his family in the country. This left us with just one more full day in London. We spent most of the morning at Trafalgar Square feeding the swarms of pigeons there. Just across the way was a big park in which workmen were digging large trenches in case of an air-raid.

We had our lunch at a nearby restaurant and then took a bus to the British museum. Along the way we noticed a long line of people waiting outside a building to be fitted for gas masks.

We spent an hour wandering through the museum. We saw the Rosetta stone, recent excavations of Ur, dating back to three or four centuries before Christ—and many other very interesting things.

Before the hour was up I began to wail to go to the cinema so the

The Edgars' house in Ashted

result was the rest of the afternoon was spent watching *Alexander's Ragtime Band.*

The next day after lunch we were on the train bound for Ashted where my father's friend, Mr. Edgar, and his family lived. We arrived at his home just in time for afternoon tea. As we drove in the long driveway leading up to the house, I got the impression that we were driving up to a mansion, but soon discovered it was not quite that, although it was a rather large house. All I could see as we went in the front door with the Edgars was a small hall with a drawing room on the left and dining room on the right.

The Edgars had three children, two older ones—a boy and a girl—and a girl my age. The younger girl, I was very disappointed to find, was away at a boarding school.

After tea (which was taken huddled around a large, log fire in the drawing room) we were taken outside for a look at the grounds, of which there were plenty. The "grounds" consisted of a beautiful bowling green at the back, a miniature golf course at the front of the house, a tennis court, a sumptuous garden, a corral in which were kept a horse and pony, and last but not least a kennel with some dogs and a few guinea pigs in it. The guinea pigs charmed me at once and I played with them till dinner time.

Just before dinner an old friend of the family dropped in and we all had dinner in a large dining room next to an open fire. The three Potters ate like horses, I'm afraid, for we were getting rather tired of restaurant meals and this home cooked one hit the spot. I hardly said a word all through the meal, but just shoveled down the food as fast as it was put in front of me, like the proverbial pig.

After dinner I sat bolt upright in a straight back chair in the dining room, not speaking unless spoken to, and listening while my father and Mr. Edgar reminisced about the "good old days" at Oxford.

When it got to be about quarter to eight, Mrs. Edgar began to look expectantly first at me, then at Mama and then at the clock and so forth back again until my mother, catching on at last, suggested that it was about time for little girls to be getting to bed. The truth of the matter was that I had not been to bed that early since we left America, but anxious to please, I followed my mother and Mrs. Edgar up the stairs, quite as if I had gone to bed at this hour every day of my life.

My bedroom was that of Frances, the young daughter at boarding school. It was a small room, but very pretty and just suited my taste exactly. Facing me as I walked in the door was a neat little bed with a flowered canopy over it and right beside it a tempting looking bookcase filled with girls' books, mostly mysteries, which made me wish more than ever that this girl Frances was home. A bureau stood against the opposite wall and in the corner on a small table stood the inevitable pitcher and wash basin. I fell asleep immediately, as I have no trouble getting to sleep in a strange bed.

5
To the Nott-Bowers at Ingatestone

It seemed I hadn't been asleep an hour when the door to my bedroom was slowly opened and a maid came hustling in with a pitcher full of ice cold water, a towel, and a washcloth. She poured the water in my own tin pitcher, placed the washcloth and towel on the stand, and then scurried out again, saying over her shoulder as she went—

"Breakfast at eight."

I watched all this with wide eyes and then when she was gone, placed one bare foot gingerly out on the cold floor. When I say simply cold, I am putting it mildly. On top of this was the icy water in that everlasting tin basin. Every time I dipped my hands into it I expected them to freeze there tightly. Strangely enough they didn't though, and after brushing the tiny icicles off my nose, I went down to breakfast.

By the time noon rolled around the sun was shining brightly and the day was warm and pleasant, so we packed up some lunch and went on a picnic. It turned out very nicely in spite of the inquisitive

The young Edgars entertained us with a picnic in the country.

ants and several other species of insects that are present at nearly
every picnic. After we had had our lunch we all had our pictures
taken and then we went home. We arrived in time for my father to
have another game of "bowls" (lawn bowling) before tea.

At tea time the talk again was all of the war and of the crisis in
England. The Edgars had friends in for tea and they seemed very
shocked that Mommy and I had not booked passage on the next
boat home. As a matter of fact, Daddy had been trying desperately
for the last few days to find a boat that had a couple of extra berths
on it, but it seemed there was no such thing. Anyhow, Mommy had
made the remark the other day, "I have a hunch we'll get to India,"
and I have noticed from long experience that everything Momma
says is apt to come true.

For the remainder of the afternoon I played outside with the dogs,
cats, and various other animals; then in the evening I sat in the
same straight-backed chair and listened to practically the same conversation. Mr. Edgar and Daddy had launched into another long,
reminiscent conversation about Oxford and tennis, and Mrs. Edgar

and Momma talked about New York and London alternately all evening long. I, as usual, remained mute except to answer a few polite questions that were put to me during the course of the evening.

Once Mrs. Edgar leaned over to me to ask, "What school do you attend, dear?" and when I told her it was just a public school not far from my home, she leaned back quite satisfied, because in England boarding schools were referred to as "public schools."

The next day was Sunday and a car ride about the country had been scheduled for the morning. Mommy, Daddy, Mr. And Mrs. Edgar, their little Scotch terriers, and I all piled in the car. We spent about two hours jaunting all over the English countryside. We drove for miles over a flat, rolling, green land, whose monotony was broken occasionally by a small English village or town.

Mrs. Edgar got out at one house and bought a dozen eggs from a large red-faced woman that came to the door. A million children peeked out from behind her apron and gazed at us with large, round blue eyes. When Mrs. Edgar was again seated in the car, Mr. Edgar started the engine motor, thus scattering the chickens that were occupying the middle of the road, and we drove back home.

In the afternoon after dinner, Peter and Betty took us on another ride, only this one was not so long and not as interesting because it took us more through the towns than through the country. Betty did some shopping and then drove us back again to the house.

Before tea time in the afternoon, Mrs. Edgar took Momma for a long walk through a beautiful stretch of woodland in the back of the Edgars' home. This (the woodland) is another thing I forgot to say that the Edgars owned.

Mr. and Mrs. Nott-Bower, good friends of the Edgars and Daddy, arrived from Ingatestone for tea at the Edgar home. We were to drive with them to their home for dinner and overnight, so when tea was over Mommy and I retired upstairs to pack our bags and also Papa's. However, looking out our window, I discovered everybody outside taking turns putting the golf ball into one of the holes, and as it looked like a lot of fun, Mommy was soon packing alone.

The drive to Ingatestone with the Nott-Bowers was a matter of only about an hour or so; therefore we arrived at their home nearly an hour before dinner.

Their house was a lovely, little semi-bungalow type with an especially beautiful little garden that had a green, green lawn.

On the inside of the house there was a long hall lined with doors on either side. The doors on the left all led to bedrooms and the doors on the right led to, in order of their appearance, drawing room, dining room, kitchen, and bathroom.

Mrs. Nott-Bower immediately took the three of us in hand and proceeded to show us to our rooms. I had been in the habit of sleeping with Momma up to now, so I got a shock when, after placing my parents in a room at the end of the hall, Mrs. Nott-Bower took me by the hand and marched me down the hall and up some narrow stairs into what to me appeared to be the attic to the bungalow.

My hostess then pointed to the door at the top of the steps and with a sweeping gesture, said triumphantly, "Here is your room," with the emphasis on the "your" as if I had been given some special privilege. The room had once been her son's when he was a small boy.

"You will not be alone, you know dear. Maria the maid sleeps right next door to you," called Mrs. Nott-Bower as she retreated down the stairs.

I turned and surveyed my small room (small to say the least). It contained simply a small iron single bed, a dresser, and three guesses what stood in the corner—of course! A wash basin and pitcher. However, since it was only one night that I would be here, I rather enjoyed the daring prospect of sleeping so far from my parents. So I trotted down the stairs, down the hall, and into the dining room where I immediately became chummy with the maid, Marie, who showed me how to set the table for dinner.

In the drawing room after dinner Mr. Nott-Bower was full of gloomy prophecies about England's crisis. He and Daddy talked at length in hushed tones, and I could only gather, by hearing my

Playing "bowls" on the green with the Edgars and Nott-Bowers.

name and Mommy mentioned several times, that they were talking over the same old subject of passage back to America.*

My little bed and I got along fine that night, except that it was very short and even with my small figure I woke up a couple of times in the night to find my toes sticking out of the covers.

When I got downstairs next morning Mommy and Daddy were already up. At six o'clock in the morning they had been awakened by Marie who had brought them "chota," which is a little pick me-up before breakfast. The English are forever eating. First they have chota, then breakfast, "elevenses" in the middle of the morning, lunch, afternoon tea, dinner, and once in a while a small snack before going to bed.

After breakfast Daddy announced that we would go back to London overnight, and pack our bags and then go on to Oxford where

---

* Mr. Nott-Bower had a small hole right in the middle of his forehead. Daddy said it was from a bullet that was fired at him during one of the battles of World War I. The bullet entered his head and passed exactly between the two lobes of the brain, leaving him alive to tell the tale.

we had planned to stay only overnight. However, now he was undetermined how long to stay before daring to cross the channel to Holland. The channel at that point, between London and Rotterdam, was decidedly unsafe.

Directly after lunch we took our leave of the Nott-Bowers and boarded a train back for London. In less than an hour and a half we were whizzing in a taxi down the left-hand side of the road toward our hotel. Along the way we noticed with a sharp pang that all the beautiful London parks were dug up in trenches.

After depositing our bags at the Strand Palace we took a twopenny bus to Trafalger Square and remained there the rest of the afternoon feeding the pigeons before returning to our hotel for dinner.

6
Oxford, the City of Bells

Ah, at last we were on our way to Oxford town! After a leisurely breakfast at our hotel we had packed most of our smaller bags, taken a taxi to a large London station, and had arrived there in plenty of time to catch our Oxford train. Now, slowly but surely we were leaving London behind and were emerging into the suburbs which gradually thinned out into green countryside. Looking out below the window of our train there was row on row of neat little houses, with compact little gardens stretching out for miles down the track.

As far as Daddy was concerned we were now approaching the climax of the whole trip. As we drew nearer and nearer our destination we could just begin to see the stately spires of Oxford appearing against a blue gray sky. That is when Daddy's eyes began to fairly shine. As closer and closer we drew the spires became clearer and clearer and finally rounded out into buildings and rich green lawns.

We stepped off the train and into the midst of Oxford life. Here we were, this was Oxford, and this was where we would stay until Daddy arrived at some definite plan of action or else until something happened that would either make us move on again or back toward America. We turned our heads to find that Daddy had disappeared again; he was off on his usual "scurries."

We stayed at the lovely old Mitre Inn on High Street or "the High" as it is called in Oxford. The inn was four hundred years old and, as Mommy said, there wasn't a level floor or ceiling in it. The floor in our bedroom sloped so that all we needed was to slide to get to the bathroom. Mommy said she was afraid it would make her sea-sick, but it didn't. However, the sloping floors and ceilings only added to the charm of the inn, and we liked it all the more for its quaint appearance. And besides that, it was almost traditional for visitors in Oxford to spend at least one night at the inn or at any rate to have a "spot of tea" before one of its blazing fireplaces.

The minute we stepped off the train Daddy was full of impatience to see his old college—Christ Church. So it was that we had barely deposited our bags in our room that we were out on the street again walking to the college which was only a couple of blocks from the inn. We entered it through the gate into Tom Quad and stood on the threshold of a beautiful grass quadrangle surrounded by grey, ivy covered buildings. Daddy was bursting to see everything at once; the high dining hall with its walls lined with portraits of famous gentlemen, classrooms, the kitchen from which had come the delicate pastries that Mommy had heard him rave about for twenty years, Christ Church meadows, and a score of other things, so the only thing to do was to take our time and spend the afternoon roaming leisurely about the campus and along the tree-shaded walks.

When we had tired of wandering in and out of the old stone buildings we started out toward the meadows. Our path led us inevitably to the beautiful college gardens. We stepped through a green arch-way into a brilliant world of sparkling colors. A tall green hedge built in a gigantic circle made us feel as if we were walking into a large round room. The garden lay next to the hedge and continued on around the circle. The center was a thick green carpet.

The flower garden was so carefully planned that each blossom seemed to blend perfectly with the next one. As Mama admitted a bit gloomily, it was beautiful.

"And I thought my rock garden was coming along so nicely before we left!" she wailed as we wended our way back to ye Mitre. On our way we stopped and fed some little fawns that poked their noses through the wired enclosure of a park.

It was a little before nine o'clock that night, after a cosy meal in a medieval dining room, that I was sent reluctantly off to bed. Hardly had my head touched the pillow than I sat bolt upright. Outside my window a wild, exhilarating sound broke loose and pealed out through the city. The cold night air was filled with the sound of a myriad of bells. Big bells and little bells, tolling the hour all over Oxford, and long after the rest had ceased, "Old Tom" kept on with its one hundred and one strokes until at last when it was all finished and the last echo had died away I slid shivering back under the icy sheets.

7
Exploring the Countryside

The next five days we drank in the sights. Drank to overflowing. I'll wager there isn't a spot in Oxford, including surrounding villages, that our inquisitive noses didn't poke into. We climbed to the bell in "Old Tom" tower; we visited Alice in Wonderland's garden and Lewis Carroll's rooms; we saw the tea pot from which Johnson drank twenty-two cups of tea each breakfast (!); we looked in on the Bodelyn Library and Christ Church library with its beautiful paintings. We went to Christ Church Cathedral and War Memorial Chapel; we saw the famous original painting at Koebler's College of Jesus knocking at the Door; we saw the nunnery where lived Rosemond, friend of King Henry VII; and on one occasion we took the bus to Iffley, where we saw an old, old Norman church. From there walked back to Oxford along the river bank (three and a half miles!). We also did a great deal of walking about Christ Church meadows and through the parks, sometimes watching a game of cricket and at another time watching two squads made up of college boys "punting" (boating) on the river.

This particular time I mention, we were walking along the river bank about a mile from the inn, when the skies opened up and we were suddenly and unexpectedly drenched with a deluge of rain. The only alternative was to seek shelter, and this we found in the form of a bridge which crossed the river. We crept under this and were soon joined by a few others who straggled in, people in a similar predicament. We were all forced to remain this way for a good three-fourths of an hour.

If this had occurred in America, by the end of this time we all would have been laughing and joking with one another, but not so here. Everyone remained quietly aloof and occupied with his own thoughts even though I thought the situation was screamingly funny. One old gentleman delicately made himself comfortable on a mud-splattered rock and morbidly watched the rain splatter on his highly polished shoes. When the rain ceased, each took his leave as matter-of-factly as he had come, as if these sudden English showers were a common occurrence and had to be tolerated as such.

One day we decided to see a bit of the surrounding countryside, so we took a bus to Wolvercote, and from there a long walk to Wytham, a completely captivating little English village which abounded in thatched roof cottages with hollyhock walks leading up to the front door.

WYTHAM

The farmer with his horse

Being a camera fiend, Daddy was in his element, for Wytham was full of marvelous picture material. It's a shame that our camera couldn't take colored pictures for everything here was color. It was like a Hollywood set with the narrow dusty little roads lined with one-storey thatched roofed houses, and then to make it more perfect, along came an old farmer sitting on top of a milk wagon drawn by a tired old horse. Daddy tried to get a picture of this, but every time he clicked the shutter, the horse would decide to move, so he finally gave it up.

We stopped at a tiny little, old inn and had a drink of "ginger beer" just for curiosity's sake. When lunch time came we walked for about a mile and finally arrived at the adorably picturesque Trout Inn. It was eight hundred years old and boasted some very old antiques and furniture. It was surrounded by a green, green lawn and had a stream running through it that was filled with some lovely little ducks. All around the lawn and under the trees were white stone benches and tables where people were sipping tea or eating lunch. We ate a leisurely meal and after about an hour hiked back to Wolvercote where we took the bus to Oxford.

8
We Meet a Knight and Visit the Allens

It was so inevitable now, whether war came or not, that our itinerary would have to be changed. We had already stayed in Oxford longer than we had planned, and there was no way of telling how much longer we would be delayed. To make up for lost time we had to cross Holland off our list. That night Daddy reluctantly sent a cable to the old Dutch gentleman's estate in Rotterdam where we had planned to spend a long weekend. Though it nearly killed Daddy, Germany also had to be taken off our list, for war or not, it was dangerous ground to be treading on. Switzerland suffered the same fate because we were only going to stop there on the way back from Germany, and going there now would only mean a needless journey which would take us quite a ways off our beaten track.

So, Daddy's carefully made itinerary was butchered rather sadly, but from France on it remained unchanged. Anyway, it all goes to show that the best laid plans of mice and men sometimes go screwy (or however the saying goes).

Each afternoon we sat around a huge log fire in the upstairs drawing room of the inn, and sipped tea while Daddy discussed the "situation" in England with some old English gentlemen. It was said that if war came, it would be only a matter of hours before the bombers would be over Britain. Prime Minister Chamberlain had gone to Hitler once while we were in London, but he had returned again unsuccessfully. And now not only the Potter family, but all England waited with baited breath for Hitler's next move. We did not have to wait long.

On the 2nd we received an invitation from Lady Wylie to come and have lunch the next day. Sir Francis had been an old school chum of Daddy's and was anxious to see him again. Almost simultaneously we were invited to Rhodes house to have tea with the Allen family whom Daddy also knew.

The luncheon was nice but passed uneventfully. Sir Francis's son met us at Christ Church gate and drove us to the house. Contrary to my vague expectations Sir Francis did not come to meet us on a white charger in shining armor, but we found him sitting quite peacefully in a rocking chair and not behaving at all as I'd always thought knights did. Apparently times had changed.

When we went to have tea with the Allens, I was awed. We walked into a beautiful entrance hall and a maid took our things. Then Mr. and Mrs. Allen appeared and announced that I would have tea upstairs in the nursery with the children. I followed a starched apron and a pair of white cotton stockings up a flight of stairs, down a hallway and emerged finally into a sunny room that had Alice in Wonderland all over the walls. Then a large woman who turned out to be a governess took me by the hand and introduced me to the two Allen children who were just about my age. They were beautiful, well-mannered children and we had a wonderful time together around the tea table. Afterwards we went outside and took turns riding a bike around the lawn. I had quite a few tumbles because I couldn't get used to the idea of having the brakes on the handlebars. When Daddy and Mommy finally came for me we were trying on the gas-masks that had been issued to the Allens and laughing at how we looked.

On the way home Daddy announced to me that they had heard a news flash over the radio while at tea that Hitler had called together a meeting of the "four powers" to Munich to discuss peace plans. The four powers being Hitler, Chamberlain, Mussolini, and De Ladier. We rejoiced. In fact, everyone looked happy—even the "bobbey" (policeman) on the corner of High Street. But some shook their heads and said, "It won't last."

That night we went to Tom Quad in Christ Church and stood alone in the deserted quadrangle listening while "Old Tom" boomed a hundred and one strokes for each original member of the college. When it was over we walked home amid the chiming of a hundred Oxford bells tolling the hour.

The next morning we left for London.

Our channel crossing could be called "The Part of our Trip Best Forgotten" or "Something to Laugh at Ten Years Hence." Daddy had crossed the channel twenty times, but this time he declared took the cake. Not one of the passengers, including the Potter trio, escaped unscathed from the awful, three-and-a-half hour trip.

That is, all except one fell victim to the rolling of the boat. This one was an old white-haired lady who sat on a bench on deck with an array of sea-sick remedies spread out on a table before her. Every fifteen minutes or so she would take a pill from one of these and pop it into her mouth. She was still sitting there when the boat landed.

9
We Arrive in France

"Attention, Monsieur, Attention! Ici, ici!" Six or seven well meaning porters made a grab at our bags and one finally winning the battle hailed a taxi and deposited us in it. The lights were going on all over the city as we drove to our hotel and I thought sleepily that the Rue de la Paix looked for all the world like Fifth Avenue, New York, and so closed my eyes to it all.

When I opened them again there we were at the St. Petersburg and from the look on Mommy's face I realized with a sigh that again she didn't approve of the quarters picked for us by Daddy. Daddy also must have seen the look (it is not a look of outward disapproval, but more one of polite resignation to fate), for he said:

"Look, Elsie, it's only for two short nights and besides the others are so danged expensive. I don't see anything wrong with it in the first place," he added.

Neither did I, but I didn't say anything as my mother can smell a rat in the most beautiful places, and she is supposed to have supreme judgment in such things.

We went up to our rooms which were quite decent looking, if old-fashioned, and went directly to bed. I woke next morning with a shriek from Mommy. We were in the same room. "I told you so, I told you so, " she cried. "Look all over me, I'm covered with little bites!"

I tried to look shocked, but indeed there were little spots all over mother's arms. She was not even paci-

fied when it was discovered that neither Daddy nor I had them. I don't know to this day what it was, but my mother always develops little spots when she doesn't approve of the hotel where we're staying.

We went to a bake shop around the corner and bought some dainty little pastry and ate it for our breakfast, after which we walked up and down wasting a lot of time until my father suggested we try to find a sightseeing bus. The best way to see Paris all in one day, he declared, was on a sightseeing bus.

That's what I like about Daddy; he is so ingenious. By the time we had located a bus it was 10:00. We boarded with several other passengers speaking several other languages and were off. For two hours we traversed all one side of Paris. Down the tree-lined Avenue des Champs-Elyses we went, past the Place de la Concord, down the Bois de Bouglogne and then first stop—the Tomb of Napoleon. Since anybody, any day can read all about these historic places in any geography or encyclopedia it seems silly to repeat the process here—so I won't. However, it is a good thing we knew a little about the places we went, because our guide who was supposed to speak French and English, generally forgot himself and spoke mostly French. So we were left standing around looking slightly bewildered most of the time.

After Napoleon's Tomb other famous places followed in quick succession (quick succession because we stopped only fifteen or

twenty minutes at each place). The climax of the morning was our
visit to the Louvre where we were allowed an hour. Instead of passing slowly as I thought it would, it passed very swiftly. We left our
little group oohing and aahing before *Mona Lisa* (you have to ooh
and aah for art's sake even if you don't like it) and "toured" by ourselves.

The one thing that stands out in my mind even above *Venus de
Milo* is the *Winged Victory*. This was really something to sigh over. It
stood at the top of a long, wide flight of stairs all by itself and it
looked so majestic that even a person knowing nothing about sculp-
turing (me) would have to pause in front of it.

In the afternoon we boarded a second sightseeing bus and toured
the other half of the city. We saw and spent half an hour at the
Cathedral of Notre Dame, stopped briefly in front of the Paris Opera
house, and visited the old Conciergerie Prison reminiscent of the
days of Louis, Marie Antoinette, and the gory French Revolution.
Our last stop of the day was at the Eiffel Tower which we viewed
with interest, but did not venture to climb. Mommy does not take
to climbing and anyhow it looked far too high and rickety.

Our bus left us at Arc de Triomphe in the Place de la Concord
and being by this time decidedly fatigued we decided to have tea on
the Bois de Boulogne. In this way we were being sensible and fashionable at the same time. What could be sweeter, especially when
we found a table empty in one of the sidewalk cafes. From here we
could view the whole world of Paris passing by.

Beautifully dressed people of wealth passed on the sidewalk or in
motors; smartly dressed women stopped for tea after a day of shopping; people on bikes rode by, and in the pathways of the mossy
woods people strolled or had picnics under the trees. And all the
while everyone chattered French excitedly (it sounded that way)
until my head buzzed.

When we were finally in bed that night we were sure we had seen
twice as much in one day as other tourists had in one week. At least
our heads and feet told us so.

We left Paris at 9:00 the next morning, but not before a slight

S. S. Excalibur

commotion. All because of Daddy's French, which consists of approximately three phrases—"Where is a good Hotel?", "Please get me a cab," and "How much do I owe you?" Surprisingly this selection did not include, "Where do I get a souvenir for my daughter?" Unfortunately for us, because it caused a slight delay. But we did finally make the train; I with a tiny green bottle of champagne attached to my charm bracelet—the souvenir.

The train took nine long hours from Paris to Marseilles. We had a compartment which held only one other occupant—a Frenchman who tried out his English on us for three hours and then fell asleep. I looked at the scenery for five hours, but finding it quite a bit like New England countryside, I followed the Frenchman's example, only waking at the large stations to hear the babble of what seemed like a million Frenchmen all talking at once.

Once our train ground to a stop and I looked out and saw a huge station with many people and porters milling around, and heard a loud speaker somewhere roar somewhat quizically—"Allo? Allo?" and then "Dee-shon." The station was Dijon.

At six o'clock we reached Marseilles and were taken to our hotel to "freshen up" and eat dinner. And what a hotel! Daddy had absolutely outdone himself to make up for the St. Petersburg Paris. The name of this hotel, or should I say palace, was the Louvre-de-la-Paix. The look of utter rapture on Mommy's face as she stepped into the beautiful lobby and practically sank knee deep into a rich wine-colored carpet was enough to repay Father a thousandfold.

"Now, this what I call a hotel," she said as an all-glass lift [elevator] bore us to our rooms.

These rooms, at least Mommy's and mine, boasted a balcony which looked right out over Marseilles harbor.

Our ship, the *ExCalibur*, was in the harbor. It will be nice to be on shipboard again and take the Mediterranean cruise, I thought. We sailed at midnight of the next day.

Part II

The Diary of June Potter,
age ten,
1938-1939

At the Arch of Ctesephon

The Mediterranean, on the Excalibur

The Mediterranean Sea is the most beautiful yet—as blue as blue can be. The ship is just *perfect*. A lovely cabin, too. The very nicest people on board. There is a girl on board who is just my age and very, very nice. Her nick-name is "J.J." She is from Siam. I know we'll have swell fun. It is lots of fun getting acquainted with every-one and everything on board. We'll stop along the way at different countries to visit. Boy, everything is just beautiful and perfect.

Oct. 10, 1938
Naples, Italy

Spent one full, glorious day in Naples, Italy. Took a taxi to Pompeii. It is a fascinating place. Street after street of old ruins of ancient Pompeii. We visited a tortoise shell factory, got trinkets before going to Pompeii.

We then went on a beautiful drive in our taxi over a 3000 ft. mountain to Amalfi. This is called the Amalfi drive and is supposed to be the most beautiful drive in the world. It certainly is!

We went all around the side of the great mountain with the beautiful blue Mediterranean with tiny ships below us. Occasionally we would pass through a small village and all the children on their donkeys would come out and wave at us. We lunched at an old monastery on the side of the mountain at Amalfi then on over to Sorento, Castelamare and Naples and back to the boat to talk over with the others what we had done that day.

POMPEII

AMALFI Drive, Italy

Oct. 11-13, 1938

On Shipboard Excalibur

Wonderful days on shipboard.
"J.J." and I have explored the ship
from stem to stern—inside and out.
We know the cook, so occasionally
we sneak down to the forbidden re-
gions of the kitchen for an apple
and lump of sugar from the tables.
Each night something is doing—movies, dances, games or some
kind of amusement. Game tournaments are going on all the time
for young and old. Every afternoon tea is served by the deck stew-
ard. "J.J." and I play many games together or just sit in our deck
chairs.

We are wonderful friends.

Oct. 13, 1938

Alexandria, Egypt

We arrived in Alexandria harbor about ten o'clock in the morning. It was my first taste of the East. Picturesque native boats were
all around contrasting with the warships, airplane carriers and
steamers from all over the world, also there.—The people on the
boat pitched pennies to the small brown boys on the pier. A magi-
cian did tricks for us. Took three o'clock train for Cairo and arrived
at the Badeaus* in time for dinner. The Badeaus took us out to see

---

* Dr. John Badeau, who was first a civil engineer, then a missionary to
  Iraq, at this time was professor of philosophy and religion at the American University of Cairo. In 1945 he became president of the University
  and in 1953 was made president of the Near East Foundation. In 1961
  President Kennedy appointed him ambassador to the E.A.R., a position
  he held until his retirement. For me, he was a kindly giant, who, after
  our visit, sent me a poem he had written about me seeing the pyramids
  for the first time, through my fingers clasped tightly over my eyes.

Jean Badeau and me

the giant pyramids and sphinx by moonlight. They were huge and looked very impressive towering up in the moonlight. We have rooms at the University of Cairo.

Oct. 14, 1928

Cairo, Egypt

We breakfasted with the Watsons. Dr. Watson then took us sightseeing all over the city. We saw the Citidel, saints' shrine at which many were worshiping, the lovely grotto with a view of pyramids, ancient Egyptian house, bazaars, museum with King Tut's treasure and wooden man thousands of years old, and more.

Had lunch with Dr. Watson* at the English Club. After lunch more sightseeing around residential part of city. Cairo is a very beautiful city. Saw the Nile with beautiful bridge over it.

Went through university, attended a tea for new members of college staff. We took an evening train back to our ship.

* Dr. Watson was president of the American University at Cairo.

Oct. 15, 1938

On Shipboard

"J.J." got off at Alexandria so I miss her quite a bit but there is so much doing all the time on ship-board that I don't miss her too much. There are loads of sports and games on the decks and in the lounge. The sea is beautiful and the boat is lovely.

We had the captain's dinner tonight. It was a swell affair, indeed. But many grown-ups got plastered.

There were paper hats and noise-makers for everyone and some-one started a chain which wound around the tables. The meal was delicious.

Oct. 16, 1938

Jaffa and Tel-Aviv

We anchored off Jaffa for about two hours in the early morning and then moved on to Tel-Aviv. We remained in the harbor for the rest of the day unloading freight. Seven complete Ford cars that were on a barge upset and sank into the sea. It was very exciting watching the divers go down after them all afternoon. We sailed in the evening.

Oct. 17, 1938

Beirut

Arrived at Beirut in the morning.—Left our boat for good this time and on to dry land again. Went to the Hotel Metropole.

Visited the American mission.* Shopped in bazaars for gifts. Had

* We began the tour of all the mission stations along the Persian Gulf for which my father was responsible. In those days these mission tours were limited to approximately one in every ten years. This was, I'm sure, be-cause of the difficulty of travel conditions in those days as well as the length of time required to get there by boat.

to go to the Turkish consul for a visa. Also had to have extra passport photo taken in order to go through Turkey on the train (without any stops) in the middle of the night! Had to wait hours in the consul.

I have lots of fun in the yard of the Hotel Metropole.

Oct. 18, 1938
Tripoli, Alleppo

Left Beirut at noon for a two-hour ride by bus to Tripoli. A beautiful drive on the very edge of the sea.

Reached Tripoli at three o'clock and took a funny little train up over the Lebanon mountains to Aleppo. From here we got on a train for an overnight trip* to Tlkochek in the desert!

Oct. 19, 1938
Mosul, Arabia

From Tlkochek we had a four-hour ride right into the desert to Mosul. It was terribly hot and dusty! We reached Mosul about three o'clock. The city looked like those in pictures rising out of the desert with tall minarets and low mud houses and walls. We had a little trouble finding a place to stay! Finally stayed overnight at Christian girls school with Mr. and Mrs. Willoughby. Had dinner at the station rest house. The trip across the desert was most interesting—camel caravans, Bedouin camps, etc. along the way. Took a night ride in a horse and buggy through the bazaar—it was just *swell*.

Oct. 20-21, 1938
Kirkuk, Arabia

Crossed the desert again (4 hrs.) to Kirkuk—much better road this time. But pretty bad anyhow. Stayed in native house with court

*In my mother's diary she wrote that the dust was so thick on the train that she could have removed it from my eyelids with a spoon as I slept.

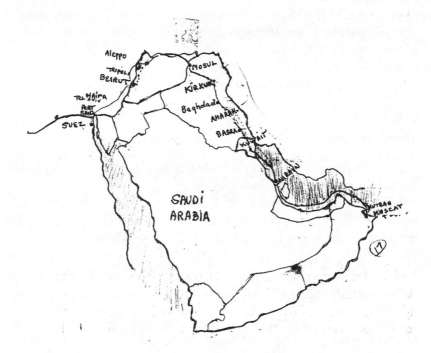

Map of Saudi Arabia with our route.

yard with Mr. and Mrs. Glessner and two children—a bit younger than I. Kirkuk* is surrounded by oil wells. In the evening we all drove out to what is called "the Gate of Hell." Gas escaping from the earth burns in flames in a circle night and day. Has been burning for hundreds and hundreds of years. I had fun playing with the girls.

Left on the night of Oct. 22 on nite train for Bagdad—scene of the *Arabian Nights*.

---

* Many of the places we visited were very remote—especially in those days. We learned later (fortunately) that on one of the desert roads we traveled, a missionary had been killed two weeks before our arrival!

Oct. 23, 1938
Bagdad, Arabia

Arrived at Bagdad early in the morning (Sunday). Hakkens met us and we stayed with them at nice house. Went to English church in morning. We went to a Bagdad bazaar and looked at a lovely Persian rug.* Bazaars are very interesting. The U.M.M. mission meeting was held at the Y.MC.A. Mr. Hakken took us out to see the great arch of Ctesiphon. It was a wonderful sight with the desert all around it.—Stayed in Bagdad three days drinking in the sights of the famous city and shopping in the bazaar.

Oct. 26, 1938
On the Train

Left Bagdad on the evening of October 26, on the night train for Basra. Such dust and dirt as I have never seen before! Kept waking up in the middle of the night with dust so thick all over us that we could have scraped it off of our pillows with a knife! But this is all part of traveling and I wouldn't have it changed for anything!

---

*   There is more to this story, as I later learned. In the bazaar my mother was very taken with the beautiful, hand-tied Bakara rug. However, after much haggling, as was the custom, both my parents finally realized that the price was too high for them to be able to afford. Sometime later that evening there was a knock on the door of the mission cottage. The rug merchant was standing outside holding the lovely rug in his arms.

"I thought you were just rich American tourist," he said. "I was quoting you oil company prices. My wife had loving care and her life was saved in your mission hospital. I can never repay that. Please take this rug as a token of my gratitude for what the mission has done."

The rug, even more beautiful in its soft colors after all these years, is on the floor of my living room in Maine.

Oct. 27, 1938

Basra

Arrived at Basra early morning of 27th. Met by Dr. and Mrs. John Van Ess and Miss Rachel Jackson. We made the Van Esses' home our headquarters for the next ten days and went on other visits from there. The home has a lovely garden of palms and such. In the evening we drove out to the new airport. It is very modernistic and has a huge, lovely, modernistic hotel right in front of it.

We were shown all over it by the manager of the hotel. Dinner with Gosslinks. Dr. Mylrea came to drive us to Kuwait day after tomorrow.

Oct. 28, 1938

Basra

Played with Ruth Gosselink, a swell girl just my age. They have a pet monkey. Played with him a lot. Played games in the house—had lunch. They have a little cart in which you can peddle all over the compound. We played with this all afternoon. Watched tennis game.

Crossing the desert

Kuwait harbor

Ate dates.

Oct. 29, 1938
Kuwait

Dr. Mylrea drove us in the morning over the desert (4 long hot hrs.) To Kuwait. Kuwait is a typical desert city. It had a mud city wall and all the houses are mud. Had lunch with Mrs. Mylrea-stayed with the Pennings. Visited the bazaar—went sight-seeing about town. Had dinner with the Pennings.

Oct. 30, 1938
Kuwait

Had lunch with Miss Van Pelt. Dr. Mylrea took us through the men's and women's hospitals. Watched tennis games on courts out in the desert. Had tea with Major and Mrs. Dixon.

Through the mail came an important looking invitation from His Highness Sheikh Ahmad al Jabir al Sabah to have dinner at his palace!

In the evening called on Captain DeGaury who has interesting old stones with Greek inscriptions.

Oct. 31, 1938

Kuwait—Dinner with the Sheikh

Today is the day we dine with the Sheikh. I was excited all day long. The gates were guarded by armed guards. All of a sudden at the top of the long flight of steps, two lights flashed on, the door flew open, and down the stairs came Shiekh Ahmad all in flowing white robes to greet us: We had dinner in European side of palace. My loose tooth came out in the middle of meal. We were intro-

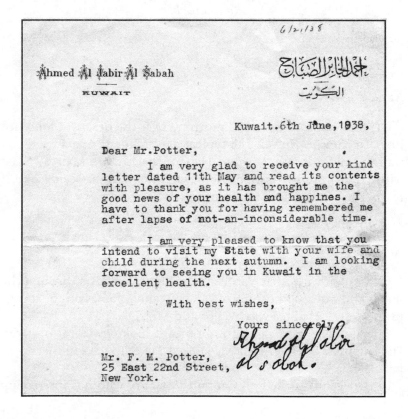

duced to the Shiekh's sons. All the *sons were introduced to us but no daughters were to be seen! Sat in drawing room after dinner and everyone drank black coffee. I sat right next to Shiekh Ahmad al Jabir al Sabah.

Nov. 1-3, 1938

Amarah

Drove back to Basra in a wild taxi (4 hrs.). Miss Dalenberg was

عبد الله الملا صالح

ABDULLA MULLA SALEH

KUWAIT 30th October كويت 38

Dear Dr.Mylrea

I have to confirm that the invitation of His Highness the Shaikh, for dinner is for to-morrow at 8 P.M. Names of the guests have been given below;

Dr. Mrs. & Miss. Potter.
Dr. & Mrs. Mylrea.
Mr. & Mrs. Pennings with their
                          son
Miss. Van-Pelt.

Yours sincerely,

[*One of those sons is the present Shiekh of Kuwait.]

waiting at the Van Esses' to drive up to Amarah. We only had time for lunch and we went right on for four more hours on the desert to Amarah. Reached the Lewis Scudders in Amarah in the evening.

Saw hospital, church and leper camp where the lepers live (was invited to tea!!). Had a picnic outside of city in a garden. Rode a camel!

Visited wonderful Amarah bazaars and bought Amarah silver. Left Nov. 3 in taxi back to Basra.

Nov. 3 and 4, 1938

Basra

Back once more to Basra for two more swell days. The Van Esses' now seems like home. Dinner at Miss Jackson's. Mom and Dad called on the Tuooni family (the boys who married American girls) but Ruth and I stayed and played in the compound. We had a lovely ride on a nice launch down the river Shatt-el-Arab.

Went on a "Bellum picnic!" and had lunch on the bank of one of the creeks among the palms-but what dirty water! Drove out through the date country. Visited a date packing plant.

Mrs. Lewis Scudder and me.

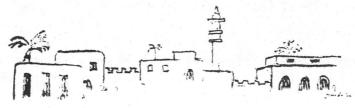

Nov. 5 and 6, 1938
Down the Persian Gulf by freighter, on the "B.I." Lines

Sailed out at four o'clock on one of the small British India lines for a two day trip down the Persian Gulf to Bahrain. Everybody came to see us off. We walked up and down the decks and Ruth, her brother and I had our pictures taken on deck.

Boy, what foul dinners that boat had! The only thing good was their rice and curry and bananas. There was also an awful steerage* on board. Mommy, Daddy and I played hearts every night. I had a good time in spite of some drawbacks.

A Bellum picnic.

* The steerage was a deck below ours. Passengers boarded with the sheep, goats and chickens which they had slaughtered on the decks in order that only freshly killed meat be eaten. This was done according to their custom.

Nov. 7, 193 8
Bahrain—9 Days

Arrived at Bahrain at five o'clock in the morning. Dr. Storm and Mr. Van Peursem met us. Got on a small launch from steamer which was anchored about five miles off shore and rode ashore just as the sun was rising over the city. We stayed with the Van Peursems on the mission compound. I took a lesson in French* every day from Mrs. Van Peursem. The water we drank was terribly salty! But, at the Storms, we had spring water.

Bahrain

We are constantly entertained at luncheons, dinners, picnics, teas, etc. by the Van Peursems, the Storms, Esther Barny, the Dames, the Bells and more.

At the tennis courts I met a lovely girl just my age who is the daughter of Mr. Bell, a wealthy oil man. She lives out in the desert in a little modern town in the middle of the desert with the families of the oil men. Went to dinner at the oil camp with Dr. & Mrs. Dane. Did not see much as it was dark.

Bahrain

Went to lunch with the Bells at the oil camp. I call it "Little

---

*   While at Bahrain I was obliged to do a lot of catching up on my school work. Mrs. Van Peursem was an excellent help here. In addition to tutoring, she gave me a French lesson every day. It would always begin with, "Je pense a quelque chose." To which I would ask, "Est ce que c'est devant moi?"

"Non."

"Est-ce que c'est derriere moi?"

"Non."

"Est ceque c'est a gauche, chaud, froid..." and on until I had acquired a fairly decent vocabulary. I loved the game.

America." It has about five broad streets with modern little houses with little front lawns on either side. The little house inside is swell. A modern little living room, dining room, 2 or 3 bedrooms, kitchen, bathroom and little porch. Mr. Bell took us all over the oil camp to oil wells, refinery, etc. It was very interesting.

Were invited to Hussein Yateem's s Arab home for a real Arab dinner. He is a rich Arab. We sat on the floor around a big white table cloth. In the center of the cloth was a whole roasted sheep—eyes and all! There were no eating utensils just hands. Mrs. Van Peursem grabbed a leg of the sheep and plopped it on my plate. The sheep's eyes were offered to Mommy but she tactfully declined. We even ate some kind of pudding with our hands. After dinner we saw some movies of Husein's.

Bahrain

Spent the day, or part of the day, at the Storms. We had dinner and tea. Went walking with Janet and her brother through the streets a bit, to a school that had real swings and seesaws. We had fun playing there with the Arab children. Janet's nurse maid or whatever you call her, went with us. Then we walked back to the house and spent a wonderful evening playing hide-and-seek in and out with the Storms' Arab butler.

*Dr. and Mrs. Storm
in their garden
Bahrain-Nov.*

Nov. 15,1938

Aboard the S.S. Barala

Boarded the *S. S. Barala*, another "B. L" lines boat for Muscat, to-day. There isn't much to do on these ships except read and walk around the decks.*

Nov. 18, 1938

Muscat

Arrived at Muscat Nov. 18. Muscat is positively the last place ever created! (So said my mother.) I will never forget sailing into that picturesque harbor. Cannons fired from shore to announce the arrival of our ship. We dropped pennies to the native boys who dived off their little canoes to get them. We went ashore in a native canoe.

From the boat all we could see were rocky mountains and an old fort. Muscat itself is nothing but low mud walls, and houses and streets just wide enough for a car. The rocky mountains that surround it radiate the sun.

Muscat

We stayed with the Dykstras. Everyday we would have prayers in the living room. The meals were very strange—boiled bananas .

There is a badminton court near the Dykstra's home—owned by the mission. Mr. Dystra took us to a little Arab home to visit. One

---

* My mother had a navy blue dress that became, for her, a very handy item. It was stylishly criss-crossed in a deep V across her front. Having an abhorrence for goat's meat, which was quite a staple along the Persian Gulf, she became adept at delicately removing the offending meat with her napkin and transferring it into the folds of her bosom. Quite a feat, but she used the technique often during our six weeks of travel in Arabia.

Muscat

of the Arab girls asked me if I'd like to climb one of the rock mountains with her. I did! !—I thought every minute I was going to fall
off and was it hot. A visitor must remain in Muscat a week as there
is no way of leaving until the next boat comes!

Saturday, Nov. 19, 1938

Mutrah

Dr. Harrison* came to take us to Mutrah for the day! Mutrah is
like a twin city to Muscat right over the mountains by the sea. So

---

*   Dr. Paul Harrison was a very colorful personality and a brilliant surgeon. During his years in Arabia, many institutions, Johns Hopkins for
one, tried to lure him back to the United States. But he remained faith-
ful to the missionary cause and to the Reformed Church mission in
particular. To me, he looked like a character out of a story book. Tall
and lanky, with a shock of hair half obscuring one eye, he had a deeply
tanned and lined face that made him look almost like an Arab himself
coming out of the desert.

    There was a government hospital not too far off, but the mission
hospital which he helped build was much preferred by Arabs and Euro-
peans alike.

Dr. Harrison* took us on this wild ride over the mountains and by the sea to Mutrah. Nothing prevented us from dropping off into the Persian Gulf!

Dr. Harrison's home was just beautiful! The upstairs had great big glass windows looking out to the sea. Before tea we watched them play tennis. We had an Arab dinner in the home of a very poor Arab. We sat on the floor to eat while goats walked in and out of the room and chickens and birds perched in the rafters!

We spent the evening in games with the Arabs in Dr. Harrison's house. Then back across that perilous ride to Muscat.

Wednesday, Nov. 23, 1938

Dr. Harrison took us on another of his wild rides in his balloon-tired car over hill and dale and rocks and boulders like a tank to a

Muscat harbor

*   Dr. Harrison was also a dynamic speaker on the occasions when he would return to the States on furlough to raise money for "his" hospital. His speeches were colorful, to say the least. He loved to describe some of the intricate operations he had performed.

As he launched enthusiastically into a very graphic description of the proceedings, on more than one occasion one or two church ladies would hurry from the room looking rather pale.

Baluchis boarding our boat en route to India.

beautiful valley for a picnic tea! It really was a lovely place end we had loads of fun. There was a little water fall right near us. Yester-day Daddy went on an all day trip into the desert with Dr. Harrison.

Saw hospital with Dr. Hosmon. I played all day with an Arab girl just my age. Had fun.

Nov. 24, 1938 (Thanksgiving)

We had Thanksgiving dinner at Mrs. Dykstra's with Mrs. Dykstra, Dr. Harrison, Dr. Hosmon and the Potters. It seemed funny having Thanksgiving there in that heat.

We sailed for India at nine o'clock Thanksgiving evening. We heard the cannons firing and we knew it was our ship, the *S. S. Barpeeta*. We were rowed out to it in a native canoe. The harbor is still pretty, even in the dark.*

---

*   Between Muscat and Karachi the *S.S. Barpeeta* stopped at several ports in Persia and Baluchistan. People would come out in little native ca-noes to board our ship. It got pretty scary a couple of times when the sea was very rough. Children were passed up to members of the crew who were swaying on rope ladders dangling over the side of the ship. Sometimes it seemed as if the heavy waves would dash them against the side of the boat.

Nov. 28, 1938

Karachii

Reached Karachii, India, late in the evening of Sunday the 27th of Nov. All we could see from the boat were lights along the wharf.

In the morning we went ashore to see the city. It was something like Cairo, Egypt. Huge camels drew tiny little carts behind them all up and down the city streets. We visited the zoo which was very fine.

We decided to change to a faster boat for Bombay. Sailed Nov. 29 on the *S.S. Vita.*

Dec. 1, 1938

Bombay, India

Spent only a few hours in Bombay—from 11:30 a.m. until 3:00 p.m. Met a former pupil of my father, Damaraj Souri, in Bombay.

Had lunch in station restaurant and then Damaraj drove us to his little home. The drive was very nice and took us through some of the fashionable parts of Bombay along the bay. At his home we met his wife and family. We left on the 3:00 train. Such a train! and what a trip overnight!! Many, many people were crowded into each car. The country was very beautiful and I really saw India for the first time—green, green padi fields; oxen drawing funny looking carts; women in bright, beautiful clothes; and big, big, wide trees.

Dec. 2, 1938

On to Vellore

Arrived at Arconem, India, 3:00 in the afternoon. Were met by Mr. Wierenga, whom we were to stay with in Vellore. After tea in the station "Uncle Casey" drove us the fifty miles into Vellore. When it began to grow dark I fell asleep.

I awoke to a great din. We were at the edge of Vellore. All Daddy's old college students were out to meet us. There we were garlanded

and after a torch-light procession consisting of a band and about five hundred people we assembled in the college compound for more garlands and speeches.

By this time the crowds numbered about one thousand! My eyes nearly popped out of my head! The Boy Scout troop even garlanded me! They made Daddy get out and march at the head of the procession.

We finally arrived at the Wierenga's home, which is the old mission bungalow (looks like the White House!). How wonderful it did look to us when we arrived at about 8 p.m.! Dr. Ida, Miss Dodd, Dr. Bernadine Sebers and Miss Dixie Scudder all came to dinner.

Dec. 3, 1938

Vellore

I woke up this morning and we all had breakfast in the dining room downstairs. I walked out on the big veranda and got a good look at my beautiful surroundings. Palm trees, cactus, green lawn, drive-way, huge compound and beautiful mountains as a background. Spent all day looking around and playing with the garlands.

In the evening Mrs. Honnegar, Miss Houghton and Mr. and Mrs. Mason Alcott came to dinner.

The Potter family

Dec. 6, 1938

Vellore

We were invited to tea at Cobb hall. It was loads of fun.

So far I have met no one my age. But the Wierengas have a son, Dick, who is four years older than I.

The compound here is beautiful and I am thrilled with the house, Vellore and all India in general.

Dec. 10, 1938

Vellore

It was "College Day" and Dr. Ida's birthday. We played sports on the lawn. Had supper on the lawn. Christmas play after. Some Indian girls dressed Mommy and I up in beautiful saris. Then we went to the play.

All the girls in colorful saris made a lovely picture. We sat cross-legged around the little pool on the college campus and the girls taught me how to eat off "planten" (plantain) leaves with my hands. Loads of fun!

Sunday, Dec. 11, 1938
Vellore

Went to Dr. Ida's* lovely home at the medical college. It is beautiful! The hall is open clear to the ceiling with big palms under the opening. There was badminton played at the college and we all watched. Had tea on the lawn. After supper we went to the lovely college chapel, where a beautiful service was held.

---

* Dr. Ida Scudder is truly a legend. During her lifetime she was honored on several occasions by the government of India and was even visited by Gandhi, who admired and respected her. As a young woman she began very humbly, however, with a one-bed clinic on the veranda of her bungalow in Vellore. The story of how she almost single-handedly raised the money and built a hospital and then a medical college for women (almost unheard of in those days, particularly in India) is nothing short of miraculous. Books and stories have been written about her, and all make exciting reading.

The medical college was one of the first of its kind to train women to become doctors. After securing permission from the surgeon general in Madras she started with makeshift equipment and herself as a principal teacher. With fourteen young women as students, she rented a hall for a lecture room, found a shed in which to do dissections, appropriated a human skeleton, and obtained permission from a local men's college, Voorhees College, to attend lectures in chemistry. She forged ahead, teaching almost all the classes herself. When the great day arrived for the students to take their final exams at the Madras Medical School, all fourteen passed, four of them with high honors.

In 1918, the Medical School for Women opened and in 1942 became a medical college. In 1947, the college finally agreed to take in male students, a decision in which my father took an active part.

Today, the Vellore Christian Medical College and Hospital has two thousand beds, serves sixty-seven thousand in-patients and over a mil-

Dr. Ida Scudder

lion out-patients a year, both at the hospital and in out-lying villages. The care given includes not only primary health care but extensive social services as well, including job training, particularly important for Indian women. Today doctors, students, and researchers from all over the world come to Vellore to study and to observe its impressive accomplishments.

My memory of Dr. Ida is that of a warm, kindly presence. More importantly though, after a long day in surgery, she would give her full attention to a game of pick-up-sticks with a ten-year-old.

Dr. Ida's house

Sunday afternoon, Dec. 11, there was a baptism in the little village outside Chittoor.

Dec. 12-16, 1938

Vellore

We came to Dr. Ida today to stay until Daddy comes back from the Madras conference.* Had the Indian girls in to dinner with games after—loads of fun. Dr. Ida loves pick-up-sticks. Mrs. A. S. Warnshius and Mrs. Horton are also staying for a day or two with us.

I spend all my days playing badminton at the college with the Indian girls. They are swell, and the medical college is beautiful.

---

*   At the time of this trip my father was chairman of the Executive Committee of the International Foreign Missions Conference of North America. In this capacity in 1938 he was selected as one of forty-five delegates from North America to attend a historic meeting of this council in Madras. The Tambaram Conference, as it was called, was an important part in all the churches of South India becoming one United Church under Indian leadership.

Vellore Medical College

Dec. 17, 1938

Vellore

Had lots of Christmas mail from home. Mommy and I sat up until 10:30 p.m. reading it.

We are going to leave Doctor Ida's for a two day visit to Chittoor.

—Did not go to Chittoor. I was taken very suddenly to the hospital with a high fever and big bump and a pain in my ear and in my throat. Dr. Ida thought at first it was mastoids. But it was a streptococcus infection. Mommy stayed in the hospital with me.

Dec. 19, 1938

Mission Hospital

Dr. Bernadine Sebers and Dr. Ida took care of me. I just love these days in this swell hospital and really feel fine in spite of the fact that everyone acts as if I were half dead. My day nurse is simply swell. She is Indian and her name is Lily. We have swell fun. My night nurse is nice too.

There are a whole lot of crows outside my window everyday and sometimes they would come through the bars in my window. One even lit on my lunch tray!

Vellore Christian Medical College campus

Vellore Hospital

Daddy came back from Madras to see me. The Wierengas came to see me and some of the mission people. One day Lazarus and his family came to see me. He has about 10 children! Mrs. Cornelius came and gave me two silver bracelets. Dr. Sebers is wonderful and lots of fun.

Lily wheeled me in to the room beside mine to visit with an old, old lady. They let me go back to Dr. Ida's on the day before Christmas.

Dec. 24, 1938

Vellore

Dr. Ida gave a Christmas party on her lawn for her servants. I handed out gifts to the children.

In the evening we went back to the hospital to see the Christmas decorations. Mommy was dressed as Santa Claus to the children in the ward and I was Santa's "Helper" in a wheel chair fixed like a sleigh! Later we had a big Christmas Eve dinner at the Wierengas'— While there Daddy arrived from Madras. After dinner we had a

Christmas tree and gifts in the drawing room upstairs.

Christmas Day!

At Dr. Ida's

   Woke up at 4:00 in the morning to watch the candle-light carol-
ers in red & green saris come from the college and circle the pond
beside the chapel.
   Woke up again about 7:00 and had (a) Christmas tree on upstairs
veranda. After "chota" we were given lots of nice gifts. In the afternoon Daddy spoke at the opening of a new village church. Later we
all went to Ranipet to Dr. Galen Scudder's for a *wonderful(!)* Christmas dinner with everyone. Late at night Mommy and I came back
to Dr. Ida's but Daddy stayed in Ranipet to go back to Madras at
early dawn.

Dec. 26, 1938

At Mrs. Honneger's

   After tea Mommy and I went to Mrs. Honniger's lovely home for
a two-day visit. It really was simply lovely! Right outside my window rose a beautiful steep mountain and every night the moon
would go down behind it. There was a school on the compound
which we visited and also a lovely chapel. Mrs. Honneger has two
huge dolls which I worshiped the whole two days. Mary Geegh was
there too. All in all we had a lovely time.

Dec. 28, 1938

At the Alcotts'

   After tea Mommy and I went on to the Alcotts' for a two day visit.
I played all the time with Margy and the two Alcott boys and also a
little Indian girl. We had swell times.
   The Indian girl taught me songs and dances all in Tamil. We all
sneaked in to an Indian wedding one day.
   Had real Indian dinner one day with our old friend Mr. Lucus.

Dec. 30, 1938

Left the Alcotts in the morning, stopping off for lunch at the Wierengas' and then boarded a train for Tindivanam. We stopped all the time and people selling things would stick their hands through our window to try to get us to buy. We bought bananas. We were six hours on the train to ride only one hundred miles!

Reach(ed) Villipouram about eight at night and were met (great to our relief) by Daddy and Mr. Cornelius DeBriun (Uncle Corny). They had just run over a cobra in the dark! They drove us on to Tindivarium about 25 miles away. Got there just in time for dinner at night. Bungalow is an old-fashioned kind—no electric lights. Lovely sleeping porch on roof. Joyce DeBriun is just my age and swell.

Dec. 31, 1938

Tindivanam

Had a reception at the De Briuns' home for the Indians. Joyce ("Juice") and I played mudpies and played all around the compound having a grand time. Did not see the old year out.

Jan. 1, 1939

New Year's day—Home mail from the boys—lovely. Went to church. Went out to a village in the afternoon—very interesting village—Nason Cornelius is working there—Saw their church and garden and had a little program afterwards. A "program" is where you sit a long time and listen to singing, or speeches—or dancing.

Jan. 2, 1939

Tindivanam

Attended a little tea at the Indian pastor's home in the afternoon— Left later to return to Vellore by car. The DeBriun family drove us all "home" to the Wierengas, as they come to the mission meeting. Everybody from all over comes to the mission meetings, so I will see all the mission children.

Jan. 3, 1939

It is good to be back at Uncle Casey's and Aunty Ella's. All is preparation for mission meetings.

Jan. 4, 1939

Vellore

Mission meeting begins.*—All the missionary families are here from all over. Joyce DeBriun, Margy Alcott and her brothers, Margaret and Francine De Valois, Bob Rottschafer, Ted Zwemer, Dick & I. We all have a grand time playing hide-and-seek all over the compound. We played tag all along the veranda.

When tea time came we had lime juice on the upstairs veranda. Daddy is sick with the same old India trouble—malaria.

Jan. 5, 1939

Vellore

More fun again today. Went to a turkey dinner at the Alcotts'. Daddy had to stay home because of his illness.

Jan. 6, 1939

Mission meetings still go on with fun for all of us (missionary children). Dinner with Miss Houghton at the hospital bungalow.

Jan. 7, 1939

50th anniversary of seminary. Daddy had to give another speech. They call it an "address." Under a big canopy on the compound we saw the movie *King of Kings*.

* This was the annual meeting of the Arcot Mission.

Jan. 9, 1939

Vellore

Shopped in the bazaar in the morning for a wedding gift. Mommy bought a table cloth. I love to go to the bazaar. There are people everywhere—hogs, cows and other animals, too. Merchants sell everything—silver, brass, fruit, sweets, and beautiful colored cloths.

In the afternoon we attended the wedding of Mr. M. Peter's daughter in Katpadi. The ceremony was in the church and was very nice. There were lots of Indian children that sat on the floor and watched. Daddy was asked to speak and give advice to the bride and groom! After the service Mommy and Daddy went to the reception. Everybody there received a paper bag with a banana, a coconut, and some betel leaf—it turns your teeth red. Horrors!

Jan. 10, 1939

Vellore

Remained at home most of the day playing around the compound. In the evening we went to Cobb Hall to hear Mr. T.Z. Koo of China speak. He was wonderful. Afterwards we went to dinner at Mrs. Honneger's. Mr. and Mrs. Adiseshiah and Mr. Van Vranken were also there.

Jan. 11, 1939

Attended last meeting of assembly in Cobb hall. Very boring! In evening we ate supper at the home of Mr. Adiesehiah. Mr. and Mrs. Gold, Dr. Ida, Miss Dodd, Mrs. Zwemer & Ted, Mr. & Mrs. Ray (Indian) & Miss Wadell also were there.

Jan. 12, 1942

Vellore

The rainy season is on—about two months late! It rains a little every day.

In the evening Mommy and I went to a supper at the Women's recreation club. It was just lovely! The Indian women were all dressed beautifully in colorful saris. I wasn't allowed to stay on to supper because of smallpox, but the entertainment beforehand was just swell, especially the fireworks at the end.

Jan. 13, 1939
Vellore

Daddy went to Madras early this morning to arrange about our passage home! But that is next month. In the afternoon one of Daddy's old college boys, Dorokano, with two friends came for tea. We all drove to the college grounds and had our pictures taken.

In the evening we attended the Boy Scout entertainment and supper at the Christian hostel. The entertainment was loads of fun! ! After that we ate supper (plough) in the courtyard. I love eating with my hands from planten (plantain) leaves. You roll the rice in a little ball in your hand and then use your thumb to plop it in your mouth.

Jan. 14, 1939
Arni

Left early in the morning with Mr. De Vries for Arni. The Arni road is just wonderful—so very Indian with carts and bullocks and people. Huge banyan trees are on either side.

Visited with the De Vrieses over Sunday.—Attended church—had tea at the minister's home—drove about the village and saw the school etc. We were given a picture of Daddy drawn by a small boy!— This is the beginning of a two weeks' tour with Miss Wedell,* visiting the entire mission.

---

* Miss Sue Weddell was part of what was called the deputation visiting the India Mission. She represented the division of Foreign Missions of the National Council of Churches.

Jan. 15, 1939

Visiting towns and villages in the Arcot Mission

Remained home all day while Daddy, Miss Wedell, Mr. De Vries & Mr. Alcott went on an all day trip to the villages.

Jan. 16, 1939

Ranipet

Mr. Van Vranken called at Arni for us and took us to Ranipet. After arriving we left soon for a trip to the villages. I love visiting the Indian villages with their little mud huts. One was particularly nice, very neat and clean. Many times we see lovely designs on the doors and walls—made with bright colors.

Had breakfast with the Van Vrankens. In the afternoon saw the girls' school, where they had a little entertainment for us. Station dinner with the Van Vrankens also. Went to the Galen Scudders to spend the night. It is very nice here.

Jan. 17-18, 1939

Ranipet, Wandiwash

Mommy went all over the mission hospital in the morning. Lovely hospital. Watched a little tennis.

Dr. Rottschafer called for us in the morning and took us for an all day trip to Wandiwash. We saw her work & the tent in which she lives! She doesn't seem to mind at all! Had lunch in the church.

In the afternoon we went to a leper village where a well-to-do citizen had given a little building for a dispensary. Daddy opened this building after our greetings in a grove of palm trees.

Jan. 19, 1939

Tindivanam

We were driven to Tindivanam by Mr. De Briun who called for us
at Wandiwash. This is our second visit to "Tindi." Arrived late in
the evening. In the morning Daddy & Miss Wedell & the De Briuns
went off to the villages. I played all day with Joyce while Mommy
read.

In the afternoon we visited the Boys High School—After the "welcome" we had tea in the school.

Jan. 20, 1939

"Tindi"

I slept late. We all went to a formal "welcoming"* in the church
escorted by the "budgemey!" (band) through the streets. Then we
were escorted back again in the same manner.

In the afternoon Mommy visited the homes of some Hindus with
the "Bible Women." Joyce and I spent the afternoon making mud
pies.

Jan. 21, 1939

Vellore

The De Briuns drove us back to Vellore early in the morning. This
is "College Day" at Voorhees College. Daddy was at college all day
visiting with old students.

Mommy and I joined them at lunch in the high school. We went
back again for tea and had our picture taken. In the evening Daddy
& Mommy went to Dr. Ida's for dinner.

*   We attended many gatherings and formal "welcomes" during our stay
        in India. The welcome address delivered by our host to the assembled,
        quite often large, gathering was frequently written out on handsomely
        decorated paper and passed around beforehand. My father would then
        bring greetings from America and then also give a formal address in
        return, answering some of their questions and concerns.

Katpadi congregation

Jan. 22, 1939
Katpadi

Sunday—In the morning we left for our second weeks' tour of the mission. Daddy preached in Katpadi church—Mommy & I joined them at the Rottschafer's for lunch and tea.

After tea Mr. Rottschafer drove us to Palamaner. The drive through the Indian countryside was beautiful.

Arrived at the Kortelings in Palamaner in the evening. It is very nice here. Miss Te Winkel's home also is sweet. She is, too.

Jan. 23, 1939
Palamaner

We visited the girls school in the morning—it was lovely. The girls were sewing. They gave me three lovely dolls—one looked like Daddy, one Mommy and the other was me.

Afterwards we saw the "monkey chaser," the big bungalow and the lovely child welfare center. I gave out candy to the children.

After lunch Mr. Korteling came to drive us to his home in Madanapalle. We visited a boys' school, a church, a Hindu girls' school and then back to the boys' school again for tea. After a beautiful drive to Madanapelli, we arrived very tired just before dinner. Had a grand dinner at the hospital bungalow.

Jan. 24, 1939
Madanapalle

We are staying with the Kortelings. It is the old bungalow that the Warnshuises lived in. There is nothing much doing except that I woke up with *awful* cramps. I guess from the strange food. Daddy & Miss Wedell went to the villages but Mom and I stayed home. Mrs. Korteling, M.D., took care of me and now I'm fine.

Jan. 25

Visited the girls' school in the morning and the hospital in the afternoon. In the late afternoon we visited the sanitarium, which is really beautiful. We do a lot of visiting.

Jan. 26, 1939
Chittoor

After lunch Mr. Korteling and "Uncle Corny" DeBruin drove us down to Chittoor. One the way we stopped in the Rajah's palace to see his elephant. We saw other wild animals but the elephant was out.

In the evening I had my first real ride in a jutka. We drove in one to the Chittoor church where we were given a very nice welcome. It is the prettiest church in the mission.

Jan. 27, 1939
Chittoor

We went to other mission bungalow to have lunch with Miss Esther De Wier. After lunch we saw the Beattie school.

The teachers of the girls school came for tea at our bungalow. In the evening we all went to Arthur John's "Ashram." Miss Wedell spoke. Mommy was bitten by bed-bugs!

After the meeting we all had dinner (Indian style) on the roof—the mosquitoes and eye-flies are terrible in Chittor!! They stick to babies' eyes, noses, and sometimes mouths.

Jan. 28, 1939

Chittoor

Mommy & I stayed close at home as there is lots of black small-pox in town. Mrs. De Velois came at nite and took us to the farm.

Jan. 29, 1939

Vellore

Had a lovely day (Sunday) at the farm with Francine and Margaret De Velois. We walked all over the farm. It is wonderful. They have cattle, chickens, and the cutest little baby goats! I held them and fed them from a bottle.

After tea Mrs. De V. drove us to Katpadi.

Jan. 30, 1939

Katpadi

Had lovely but quiet day at the Rottschafers. After tea Mrs. Rottschafer drove us to Vellore. Daddy & Miss Wedell were out most of the time visiting villages.—It is to *grand* to be back at the Wierengas' after our two weeks' tour of the mission. It is like home.

Jan. 31, 1939

Went to a very nice Indian tea at the home of one of Daddy's old students. There were about seventy people present. We had tea on tables on the lawn.

Miss Wedell is staying with the Wierengas' too.

Feb. 2, 1939
Vellore

Had second mission meeting today at the Mason Alcotts. All the mission were there. Did not get home till late at night (for dinner).

Feb. 3, 1939
Vellore

Mommy & I stayed home most of the day. But there is always something to do. I sat on the wall by the Arni road and watched everything.

Feb. 4, 1939
Vellore

In the evening Mommy and I went to a little entertainment at the Women's Recreation club. The little show was swell—mostly for children. An Indian girl did a beautiful Indian dance.

The women's jewels and saris were beautiful! I did not remain for dinner on the roof.

The DeBriuns with Mom and me.

Feb. 5, 1939

Vellore

Sunday—We did not go to the Tamil Church in the morning, but went to the chapel at College Hill in the evening. Miss Wedell was the speaker. Afterwards we rode out to the water tank to see the full moon.

Feb. 6, 1939

Vellore

We're all excitement now because we are thinking of starting home in about two weeks! Miss Wedell left Vellore today for the north and then Arabia. We all drove at noon to Katpadi to say "goodbye." Again, we went to the tank to see full moon in the evening. This time we drove around the fort.

Weyerhausen Chapel on campus

Feb. 7, 1939
Vellore

Nothing special happened today. We just sat on the veranda and read. Daddy goes to meetings all the time! I read *The Wizard of Oz*. It is absolutely my most favorite book.

Feb. 8, 1939
Vellore

We remained home till after tea. Then we visited the silver bazaar to get me a trinket or two and get Mommy's glasses chain fixed.

The silver bazaar is nice. I got a charm for my bracelet. It is the goddess Laksmi.

Feb. 9, 1939

Vellore

Mommy and Uncle Casey and I play carroms [a game] all the time. Auntie Ella has gotten another bike and let me use it. I have no end of fun. I will never forget these wonderful days riding all over the lovely compound on the bike. Today I got a little "woozy" because I rode around at mid-day without my topee [sun hat].

Feb. 10, 1939

Vellore

Nothing special during the day. Dick and I play. After tea every day I have a grand time riding Auntie Ella's bicycle. In the evening Auntie Ella, Mommy, Uncle Casey and I went to a show at Cobb Hall.

Feb. 11, 1939

Vellore

In the afternoon Mommy and I went to Francine de Valois's birthday party at the farm. Lovely party. Picked up the dear little goats again—in my pink silk dress! Mrs. de Valois wants me to spend a few days with Francine and Margaret but Mom is afraid of the snakes and scorpions in the fields. In the evening we went with some others to dinner at Mr. Lucas's.

Feb. 12, 1939

Vellore

It is "Hospital Sunday" here. In the evening we attended church at the Fort church. Dr. Galen Scudder was the speaker. Afterwards

There will be

A Public Meeting

on Friday the 17th February '39 at 6 : 30 p. m.

AT

The Voorhees College, Cobb Hall

to bid good-bye to

Dr. & Mrs. F. M. Potter

Members of the Deputation, Board of Foreign
Missions R.C.A.

You are very cordially invited to be present.

COMMITTEE.

Dr. Ida. S. Scudder.

Dr. R. P. Nathanial.

Mr. S. J. Savarirayan.

„ H. P. Thomas.

„ Daniel Isaiah.

„ C. J. Lucas.

Rev. S. Ponnurangam.

VELLORE.

16—2—39.

American Arcot Mission Press, Vellore.

Central court of the medical college

all the Ranipet people came to the Wierengas' for dinner. It is Lincoln's birthday but no one seems to notice, here!

Feb. 13, 1939
Hospital Day

We all went to the hospital in the afternoon for tea on the lawn and a show on the compound later in the afternoon. That Indian girl did that wonderful dance again. Made friends with Indian girl named Sandari. We saw Lazarus and said "good bye" to him and his *eleven* children.

Feb. 14, 1939
Katpadi Farm

Spent a wonderful day with the de Valoises at the farm. In the evening we all, Wierengas too, had dinner with Mr. Santosh and his wife. It was a real Indian dinner—with rice and curry. We ate sitting on the floor with our fingers off plantain leaves. They gave me a beautiful beach bag which Mrs. Santosh has made for me.

Feb. 15, 1939

Vellore

Started *packing* for home!!! Imagine!
Went to the bazaar in the evening and
shopped a bit.

Feb. 16, 1939

Vellore

Helped pack in the morning. We went to wonderful Indian dinner of plough at the home of a Brahmin, Natesa Ayiar. It was on
the roof under the sky.

Feb. 17, 1939

Vellore

Had tea with Mrs. Honneger and afterwards called on Mrs. Tomas
Harris. Spent most of the evening getting ready for our departure!
It doesn't seem possible that we are leaving tomorrow.

Feb. 18, 1939

Homeward Bound

The Day of Departure has come!!! Uncle Casey drove us to
Katpadi. Took good long looks at Vellore going out. Passed old
Hindu procession on the way to station. Almost all the mission
were at Katpadi to see us off. In Madras several of Daddy's old students were at the station to meet us. We had tea together in the
station and Srineasen let us have his car and driver for the afternoon. We went about window shopping and then had tea with Mss
Alice Van Doren at St. Christopher's College. The whole crowd (the
college boys and Miss Van Doren) came to the station to see us off
on the night train. What a train!— What a night!

Feb. 19, 1939

Madura

Bannigar met us at the station and took us to her home for over
night. Had a nice restful day. After tea we drove to see the Madura
Temple. It was interesting but horrible!* Daddy spoke in the college chapel in evening. Friends came in for dinner.

Feb. 20, 1939

Mrs. B. drove us to the station and we started our second day and
night of train travel to Columbo. Not too bad a trip to the boat.
Crossed over to Ceylon about sunset. Didn't get sea-sick. Such a
wild night as we had in the train! ! ("Call me Jacob!!"*) We would
wake up about every hour to find ourselves in a strange dimly
lighted station and hearing people calling out strange Indian words.
I kept rolling off on to the floor of our compartment. The bed bugs
were terrible. Reached Columbo early the next morning. Stayed at
the Y.W.C.A.

Feb. 21, 1939

Columbo

Columbo is simply beautiful! It is really the luxuriant tropics.
Palm trees and blue water everywhere. Went riding about city in
the morning. We went shopping for curios and ended up by buy-
ing ourselves a teakwood chest! I got a lovely moonstone necklace.

In the afternoon we took a train for a lovely trip to Mt. Levinia—
I had my first ride in a rickshaw. Mt. Levinia is lovely! We had tea at

---

*   I remember that this was my first experience of seeing an exception-
ally deformed beggar.

*   My father must have read me the story in Genesis, because I was refer-
ring to the passage in the Bible where Jacob slept on a stone for his
pillow.

the hotel and walked on the rocks and watched people swimming. The palms reached way out over the water. Strange boats were docked on the beach. When we got back I had my first long nap. Bought several curios.

Feb. 22, 1939

Columbo

We were up early and off to our ship, the *Dempo* (Rotterdam Lloyd Line). We bought two lovely little Ceylon boats from the deck of our ship. The men send them up to the decks by a bag and ropes. Sailed at 11 A.M. on our homeward journey. The *Dempo* is a very large boat. With separate dining room and play room for children— (me).

Feb. 22 to Mar. 2

S. S. Dempo

Had ten wonderful days at sea. The Indian Ocean and Red Sea were as calm as a mill-pond. The boat is really lovely. We traveled 2nd class and it was just fine—lots of lovely parties—particularly for us children. All of the parties and sports were shared with the first class. I was very hot for the first three or four days out of Columbo. But, by the time we reached Port Said it had grown very cold. I had four friends, two boys and two girls—particularly one girl. All four were English. We had

wonderful times together. We would play ping pong & other sports in the daytime & walk the deck and talk in the evening. There was also a Dutch girl about my age on the boat, but we couldn't understand one another.

Enjoyed so much sailing through the Suez Canal. The wind was so strong that it blew the stern of the ship around into the mud and for about 10 minutes we were aground. On either side of the Suez there were long stretches of desert as far as we could see. We reached Port Said at 11 P.M. on March 2. We remained overnight on the boat.

Mar. 3, 1939

Egypt Re-visited

Went ashore at about 9:00 in the morning. Most of the time until lunch was taken up with customs and American express men. We had lunch at a funny little place—"The bill was terrific!" said Daddy. Took the train in the afternoon for Cairo. Reached Cairo in time for tea with the Badeaus. Had dinner with Badeaus also.

Daddy and Mommy are sleeping at the American University of Cairo and having lunch and dinner with the Badeaus. I am staying with the Badeaus the whole time. Jean and I are having a simply *wonderful* time together. We play all day long—around the house and around the block. We go to the "Grotto" almost every day and play all around the caves.

Mar. 4, 1939

We went with Dr. Badeau, Jean, and Roger out to Sakkara to see the Step Pyramid, and some of the old tombs. The Step Pyramid is about 700 years older than the Great Pyramid. We took a picnic lunch and stayed until afternoon. Dr. Badeau took us into all of the old tombs. If they were too dark Mommy stayed outside while we went in. She only likes light tombs.

In some places we would have to crawl along on our hands and

Outside Cairo, on second visit en route home to U. S.
"Mommy only likes light tombs."

knees through narrow tunnels. We rode around the tombs on camels and donkeys.

In the afternoon Mrs. Badeau had some friends in for tea to say
"goodbye" to Mrs. B.'s mother, who was going with us to America.

Mar. 5, 1939

Cairo

Sunday—In the morning we attended the English service at the
cathedral. It was a lovely place. We had lunch with Dr. & Mrs.
Watson at the university. In the afternoon we drove with Dr. & Mrs.
Badeau and family out to see the great pyramids and Sphinx by
daylight. After a slight shower it was a lovely afternoon. When we
reached the pyramids there was a lovely rainbow arching over them.
We all rode donkeys to the Sphinx!

Had supper with the Badeaus. In the evening Daddy preached at
the mission church or rather the American Church.

Mar. 6, 1939

Cairo

In the morning Mrs. Badeau, Mommy, and I went shopping in the bazaar for gifts to bring home to the boys. The Cairo bazaar is just grand. We spent far too much money, but we wish we could have spent more. After lunch Mommy, Mrs. Badeau Sr., Jean, and I went to the "Grotto." I never tire of going there. It is beautiful with the big artificial cave and park. Jean and I rode a swan boat on the lake.

In the evening Mommy and Daddy went to dinner at the Wilbert Smiths. They used to know them at Kodai. I stayed home with the Badeaus.

Mar. 7, 1939

Alexandria

Starting home today on the last lap of our trip. Left Cairo for Alexandria at 9:30 A.M. There were quite a few people at the station to see Mrs. Badeau off. She is traveling on the same boat with

Visiting Athens on return trip to the U.S.

us. Dr. and Mrs. B. Jr. came all the way to the ship with us. We had
sandwiches and tea on the train. When we reached the boat we all
had tea aboard together. We had a lovely letter from each of the
boys. It will be swell to see the boys again. How nice it is to be back
on the *Export* boat.

It is just like the *ExCalibur* but with different people. We sailed at
midnight.

Mar. 8, 1939

The Mediterranean; On the S. S. Excambion

It was rough almost immediately after we sailed. So rough today
we could hardly stand. We have all gone to the dining room for
each meal but alas, no one has any appetite! Early to bed tonight. It
was so rough all night that I crawled into bed with Mommy. The
wind was awful and seemed as if it would blow the boat to pieces. I
hope it is calmer tomorrow so that I can sit up and take notice of
things.

Mar. 9, 1939

At Sea—Athens, Greece

Much calmer this morning, thank goodness!

At noon we landed at Piraeus, the port of Athens. Mrs. Badeau
and Mr. Mack joined us in a taxi and drove us to Athens. It was
wonderful. We visited the Acropolis and Parthenon, Mars Hill, and
the prison of Socrates. I never get tired of visiting historic old ruins. I love it. We also saw many other places of interest. I love Athens. I don't blame Daddy for talking so much about it!

We sailed from Piraeus in the evening.

Mar. 10, 1939

At Sea

Today is Daddy's birthday. The sea was calm this morning, but
in the afternoon it blew up rough again. At meal times I notice that

a girl with pigtails and about my age walks in and sits at the table right next to us. I smile at her and she smiles at me. On deck we met and got acqainted. I am so glad to have someone here to play with. She is nice and a character if I do say so. We all play deck sports and ping pong all the time.

Mar. 11, 1939
Naples, Italy

We passed Stromboli about eight o'clock this morning. Sara Sebury (the girl's name) and I played ping pong and in the lounge until late afternoon. Then we reached Naples, Italy. We took a taxi to the glove shop where Daddy and I bought gloves. From there we went shopping elsewhere. We bought an Italian doll for my collection and a lovely cameo for Mommy. The little shops were beautiful.

Then back to the ship and more fun with Sara.

Mar. 12, 1939
Naples

Went ashore and drove in a cute little carriage to visit the cathedral and the museum. Naples seems like such a nice city—so very clean.

In the afternoon we took a carriage again and visited the aquarium. I love the rides in the carriages. But it was awfully damp and cold. We sailed in the evening.

Mar. 13, 1939
Pisa and Leghorn

Reached Leghorn about noon. Took a taxi for a 15-mile drive to Pisa. The Italian country is just lovely—the flat farmlands near the sea and the snow-capped mountains in the distance. We all climbed the leaning tower at Pisa and visited the cathedral and baptistry.

Then we drove back along the shore through Lido, etc.

Mar. 14, 1939

Genoa

Reached Genoa in the early morning. We will remain here for two days.

In the afternoon visited the cemetery and saw the *beautiful* marble statues for which the city is noted. The statues were really *beautiful*. The city is built on the side of a mountain and is very quaint. We shopped in the cutest little shops in the still cuter little streets. Hardly more than alleys on the side of the hill.

Mar. 15, 1939

Genoa

Shopped some more in the morning. In the afternoon we sailed.

Mar. 16, 1939

Marseilles

Reached Marseilles today. We shopped a little in the afternoon but it was so cold and windy that we were glad when we got back to the boat.

Mar. 16 - 27, 1939

Marseilles to Boston

Eleven grand days on the sea. Sara and I have simply wonderful times together. We did the usual exploring of the ship but with Sara it was even more extensive exploring than I ever did. We played, too, the usual decks sports and games. There is a little boy called Barrett Churchill on this boat about 1 1/2 years old who I take care of every day. What a trial! ! ! But he is awfully cute! And actually really fun, too.

Also on this boat is a lovely young Englishman named Mr. Cecil Burns. He and I play ping pong EVERY day. We have loads of fun and I always beat him! On one dance on the boat he even asked me for a dance.

We had a masquerade ball on board and I won a prize for the most beautiful costume (Indian sari), and Sara won one for the most original (Tom Sawyer).

Daddy took a prize in a ping pong tournament and Mommy took a prize at nothing! Played lots of shuffleboard.

Mar. 22, 1939

At Sea

It was Mommy's birthday and Daddy and I had the ship's chef make her a lovely cake!

Two or three days were very rough although none of the Potters were sick. One night the wind and waves were so bad that two huge windows about an inch thick were smashed in and our verandas were flooded with water. And I slept through it all. Imagine.

Mar. 27, 1939

Boston

Reached Boston-U. S.A. safe and sound this morning. Went ashore in the afternoon on good old terre firma once again. Daddy bought a new hat! Afterwards we went and I saw the Bunker Hill monument for the first time.

Mar. 28, 1939

Boston to New York

Left Boston today for good old New York and the boys! I can't believe that tomorrow we will actually be home after seven months away. Packing most of the day. It is cold and stormy outside.

Mar. 29, 1939

New York 10 A.M.

Sailed slowly into the Hoboken (ICJ) pier. (Mr. Burns looked at the N.Y. skyline.) We met the boys at ten o'clock on the Hoboken pier. Had the loveliest reunion possible!!! Aunt Bunny and the three Ebys and Uncle Banie and the entire Ruegger family were all there to meet us, too!

Had lunch at the Rueggers and dinner with Aunt Florence and Uncle Banie and family. After a visit from the Fairweathers we went to New Brunswick to live for two months in the house on the campus of the New Brunswick Seminary which is kept for missionaries on furlough.

The End.

Epilogue

In the years after this diary was written (fifty-four years!) life took over and crowded out thoughts and memories of my childhood trip along with any possibility, I thought, of ever seeing those far-away places again. Then, quite unexpectedly, something happened to cause that to change.

My youngest daughter, Lisa, on a travel fellowship abroad, through a strange set of circumstances found herself in the south of India not too far from where I had stayed as a child.

And so, my childhood diary and the pictures were uncovered in the attic, and some weeks later in May of 1992 a brand new diary was begun as I traveled to visit all the places, smell the aromas, absorb the colors, and eventually stay in the same house in which I had lived in 1938, this time seeing it with my own daughter.

The following excerpt from my 1992 diary begins as we left Kodaikanal. The road from Kodaikanal was a thirteen-hour trip to Vellore; two hours down the seven thousand foot mountain and then eleven hours across the plains in over one hundred degrees heat. In my diary I wrote:

> We (Lisa and I) left at 7:00 A.M. to begin the hair-raising descent down the mountain to the hot plains below. The journey is not for the faint hearted. The narrow road is treacherous, punctuated intermittently by piles of rubble and full of hairpin turns.
>
> There was nothing to separate us from the drop-offs of thousands of feet to the valley below. Buses, motorcycles, trucks, and small cars like ours careened down the "ghat," honking and missing each other by inches. When we reached the plain at 9:30 A.M. more thrills were to follow.
>
> Our drivers, brothers, talked continually in Tamil as we wove in and out of traffic, gesturing excitedly as they did so. They were young and full of vim and vigor—not a good trait

behind the wheel in India. They also, the driver especially, could hardly take his eyes off Lisa. We wished he were this dedicated to the road ahead. On this thoroughfare, all the vehicles play the game of "chicken." We would travel at a good clip honking vigorously, aiming directly at an oncoming car until one finally gave way at the very last minute, always missing the other auto or bus by, literally, inches. It was soon apparent that one brother was the most daring "chicken" player. In vain we begged him to slow down, but his agreement wouldn't last five minutes before we'd be off again at breakneck speed. Forty-five miles per hour is breakneck when one is dodging cows, old men, children, buses, and lorries!

The long, dusty road, lined mostly with banyan and eucalyptus trees, offered such a variety of sights and sounds that despite the intense heat and wild driving, I was totally captivated. We passed tiny villages filled with people; beautiful, graceful women in brilliantly colored saris carried huge burdens on their heads, either shiny brass water jars, sacks of meal, or firewood; little children played with one another, the big ones carrying or caring for the little ones; mothers bathed babies with pitchers of water; old men sat or squatted in the shade. Bullock carts, whose animals had brightly painted horns, vied for their place in the traffic. Often large herds of bison or goats caused us to stop and steer cautiously around, thus greatly vexing our driver.

We only stopped once to fill our tank with gas and avail ourselves of the dreaded native toilet found in the shed in back of the station. In spite of the heat it was a pleasure to have a few moments of relief from the continual honking of our car's horn. It was also gratifying to stretch our legs. The aroma of strange spices mingling with the smell of cow dung was wafted to us from a nearby village. Not an unpleasant odor, but one which we had only been faintly aware of through the open windows of our small car. All of these sights, sounds, and smells seemed unchanged from when I was last here over fifty years ago.

As we began to near the area of Vellore the banyan trees seemed to be more massive and the terrain rockier. Finally, in the distance, there appeared hills consisting mainly of large boulders, displaying little vegetation, unlike the green mountains we had just left. Then somehow, from some long forgotten memory, I recognized those hills and knew that we were nearing Vellore.

It was dark when we finally reached our destination, which turned out to be none other than Dr. Ida's home, now a guesthouse for visitors from all over the world. There was the entrance hall just as I remembered, open to the night sky and filled with palms and other lush tropical plants. The interior was heaven after our arduous journey. The walls, built entirely of huge blocks of concrete, and the whirring fans above made the whole area cool and inviting. I was a child again as I looked around and absorbed all the familiar sights. That is until one of our young drivers, putting down our suitcases, turned to Lisa and said, "Why do you have your mother take this lengthy day trip in the sun? She is too aged!"

Have I become this old so soon?